W9-APR-818

GAIL BORDEN
Public Library District
270 N. Grove Avenue
Elgin, Illinois 60120
(847) 742-2411

JUNIOR DRUG AWARENESS

Alcohol

JUNIOR DRUG AWARENESS

JUNIOR DRUG AWARENESS

Alcohol

Terri Peterson Smith

CHELSEA HOUSE
PUBLISHERS
An imprint of Infobase Publishing

Junior Drug Awareness: Alcohol
Copyright © 2008 by Infobase Publishing

All rights reserved. No part of this book may be reproduced or utilized in any form or by any means, electronic or mechanical, including photocopying, recording, or by any information storage or retrieval systems, without permission in writing from the publisher. For information, contact:

Chelsea House
An imprint of Infobase Publishing
132 West 31st Street
New York NY 10001

Library of Congress Cataloging-in-Publication Data

Smith, Terri Peterson.
　Alcohol / by Terri Peterson Smith.
　　p. cm.—(Junior drug awareness)
　Includes bibliographical references and index.
　ISBN 978-0-7910-9764-9 (hardcover)
　1. Drinking of alcoholic beverages—United States—Juvenile literature.
　2. Teenagers—Alcohol use—United States—Juvenile literature.
　3. Alcoholism—United States—Juvenile literature.　I. Title.　II. Series.

　HV5066.S45 2009
　613.81—dc22　　　　　　　　　　　　　　　2008014066

Chelsea House books are available at special discounts when purchased in bulk quantities for businesses, associations, institutions, or sales promotions. Please call our Special Sales Department in New York at (212) 967-8800 or (800) 322-8755.

You can find Chelsea House on the World Wide Web at
http://www.chelseahouse.com

Text design by Erik Lindstrom
Cover design by Jooyoung An

Printed in the United States

Bang NMSG 10 9 8 7 6 5 4 3 2 1

This book is printed on acid-free paper.

All links and Web addresses were checked and verified to be correct at the time of publication. Because of the dynamic nature of the Web, some addresses and links may have changed since publication and may no longer be valid.

CONTENTS

Battling a Pandemic: A History of Drugs in the United States

When Johnny came marching home again after the Civil War, he probably wasn't marching in a very straight line. This is because Johnny, like 400,000 of his fellow drug-addled soldiers, was addicted to morphine. With the advent of morphine and the invention of the hypodermic needle, drug addiction became a prominent problem during the nineteenth century. It was the first time such widespread drug dependence was documented in history.

Things didn't get much better in the later decades of the nineteenth century. Cocaine and opiates were used as over-the-counter "medicines." Of course, the most famous was Coca-Cola, which actually did contain cocaine in its early days.

After the turn of the twentieth century, drug abuse was spiraling out of control, and the United States government stepped in with the first regulatory controls. In 1906, the Pure Food and Drug Act became a law. It required the labeling of product ingredients. Next came the Harrison Narcotics Tax Act of 1914, which outlawed illegal importation or distribution of cocaine and opiates. During this time, neither the medical community nor the general population was aware of the principles of addiction.

After the passage of the Harrison Act, drug addiction was not a major issue in the United States until the 1960s, when drug abuse became a much bigger social problem. During this time, the federal government's drug enforcement agencies were found to be ineffective. Organizations often worked against one another, causing counterproductive effects. By 1973, things had gotten so bad that President Richard Nixon, by executive order, created the Drug Enforcement Administration (DEA), which became the lead agency in all federal narcotics investigations. It continues in that role to this day. The effectiveness of enforcement and the so-called "Drug War" are open to debate. Cocaine use has been reduced by 75% since its peak in 1985. However, its replacement might be methamphetamine (speed, crank, crystal), which is arguably more dangerous and is now plaguing the country. Also, illicit drugs tend to be cyclical, with various drugs, such as LSD, appearing, disappearing, and then reappearing again. It is probably closest to the truth to say that a war on drugs can never be won, just managed.

Fighting drugs involves a three-pronged battle. Enforcement is one prong. Education and prevention is the second. Treatment is the third.

Although pandemics of drug abuse have been with us for more than 150 years, education and prevention were not seriously considered until the 1970s. In 1982, former First Lady Betty Ford made drug treatment socially acceptable with the opening of the Betty Ford Center. This followed her own battle with addiction. Other treatment centers—including Hazelden, Fair Oaks, and Smithers (now called the Addiction Institute of New York)—added to the growing number of clinics, and soon detox facilities were in almost every city. The cost of a single day in one of these facilities is often more than $1,000, and the effectiveness of treatment centers is often debated. To this day, there is little regulation over who can practice counseling.

It soon became apparent that the most effective way to deal with the drug problem was prevention by education. By some estimates, the overall cost of drug abuse to society exceeds $250 billion per year; preventive education is certainly the most cost-effective way to deal with the problem. Drug education can save people from misery, pain, and ultimately even jail time or death. In the early 1980s, First Lady Nancy Reagan started the "Just Say No" program. Although many scoffed at the program, its promotion of total abstinence from drugs has been effective with many adolescents. In the late 1980s, drug education was not science-based, and people essentially were throwing mud at the wall to see what would stick. Motivations of all types spawned hundreds, if not thousands, of drug-education programs. Promoters of some programs used whatever political clout they could muster to get on various government agencies' lists of most effective programs. The bottom line, however, is that prevention is very difficult to quantify. It's nearly impossible to prove that drug use would have occurred if it were not prevented from happening.

In 1983, the Los Angeles Unified School District, in conjunction with the Los Angeles Police Department, started what was considered at that time to be the gold standard of school-based drug education programs. The program was called Drug Abuse Resistance Education, otherwise known as D.A.R.E. The program called for specially trained police officers to deliver drug-education programs in schools. This was an era in which community-oriented policing was all the rage. The logic was that kids would give street credibility to a police officer who spoke to them about drugs. The popularity of the program was unprecedented. It spread all across the country and around the world. Ultimately, 80% of American school districts would utilize the program. Parents, police officers, and kids all loved it. Unexpectedly, a special bond was formed between the kids who took the program and the police officers who ran it. Even in adulthood, many kids remember the name of their D.A.R.E. officer.

By 1991, national drug use had been halved. In any other medical-oriented field, this figure would be astonishing. The number of people in the United States using drugs went from about 25 million in the early 1980s to 11 million in 1991. All three prongs of the battle against drugs vied for government dollars, with each prong claiming credit for the reduction in drug use. There is no doubt that each contributed to the decline in drug use, but most people agreed that preventing drug abuse before it started had proved to be the most effective strategy. The National Institute on Drug Abuse (NIDA), which was established in 1974, defines its mandate in this way: "NIDA's mission is to lead the Nation in bringing the power of science to bear on drug abuse and addiction." NIDA leaders were the experts in prevention and treatment, and they had enormous resources. In

1986, the nonprofit Partnership for a Drug-Free America was founded. The organization defined its mission as, "Putting to use all major media outlets, including TV, radio, print advertisements and the Internet, along with the pro bono work of the country's best advertising agencies." The Partnership for a Drug-Free America is responsible for the popular campaign that compared "your brain on drugs" to fried eggs.

The American drug problem was front-page news for years up until 1990–1991. Then the Gulf War took over the news, and drugs never again regained the headlines. Most likely, this lack of media coverage has led to some peaks and valleys in the number of people using drugs, but there has not been a return to anything near the high percentage of use recorded in 1985. According to the University of Michigan's 2006 Monitoring the Future study, which measured adolescent drug use, there were 840,000 fewer American kids using drugs in 2006 than in 2001. This represents a 23% reduction in drug use. With the exception of prescription drugs, drug use continues to decline.

In 2000, the Robert Wood Johnson Foundation recognized that the D.A.R.E. Program, with its tens of thousands of trained police officers, had the top state-of-the-art delivery system of drug education in the world. The foundation dedicated $15 million to develop a cutting-edge prevention curriculum to be delivered by D.A.R.E. The new D.A.R.E. program incorporates the latest in prevention and education, including high-tech, interactive, and decision-model-based approaches. D.A.R.E. officers are trained as "coaches" who support kids as they practice research-based refusal strategies in high-stakes peer-pressure environments. Through stunning magnetic resonance imaging (MRI) images, students get to see tangible proof of how various substances diminish brain activity.

Will this program be the solution to the drug problem in the United States? By itself, probably not. It is simply an integral part of a larger equation that everyone involved hopes will prevent kids from ever starting to use drugs. The equation also requires guidance in the home, without which no program can be effective.

Ronald J. Brogan
Regional Director
D.A.R.E America

1

Conflicting Voices

"**D**on't drink. It's against the law."

"You'll get kicked off the team if you are caught with alcohol."

"C'mon, have a beer. You won't get caught."

"Drinking can make you sick, or worse."

"All of the popular people are drinking."

Our culture is full of mixed messages about alcohol. For example, alcohol advertisements say to "drink responsibly." At the same time, they try to show that drinking is a lot of fun. Alcohol companies do this because they are trying to make money. If they make drinking look like fun, they will get more people to buy alcohol. In the ads, good-looking and popular people are shown drinking. Ads seem to say, "Do what they do—drink alcohol—and you can be like them."

There are also mixed messages about how old people must be in order to drink alcohol. The legal age for drinking is 21 in the United States, but many people younger than that drink anyway. While it's illegal to sell alcohol to anyone under age 21, it is reported that young buyers make up a quarter of alcohol sales in this country. Beer and other drinks sometimes flow at many teen parties. It can seem like drinking is the way to be included and fit in with the most popular kids, legal or not.

Even parents can give mixed messages. They tell their children to not drink, but kids see their parents and other adults having alcoholic drinks at parties, sports events, and other celebrations. Some parents "look the other way" when their teens drink, and view it as just part of growing up. A few even supply alcohol for their teens' parties. "They're going to drink anyway," some parents might say to themselves. "At least they're doing it at home and not out driving somewhere."

In the end, the decision to drink or not to drink is up to each person. The best way to make good decisions about drinking is to have all of the information about alcohol—the problems it can cause, how it works in your body, and how to turn down alcohol in the face of peer pressure, advertising, and the stresses of life.

THE MOST POPULAR DRUG

It is important to know that alcohol is a drug. That may seem surprising, since people don't need a note from the doctor to get it. And it's not the kind of drug that dealers sell on street corners. Alcohol is a legal drug for people over age 21 and they can easily buy it at a store— sometimes even a regular grocery store. Alcohol is the most widely used drug in the United States.

There are many different substances that are called alcohol. The kind in beverages is called ethyl alcohol.

THE MYTHS OF ALCOHOL

Myth: "I'll be careful and in control."

Truth: The more you drink, the less control you have. After a few drinks, you become less and less able to make good decisions. This includes decisions about how much alcohol you think you can handle.

Myth: "Everybody does it."

Truth: In a survey given by the Partnership for a Drug-Free America, 31% of teens said they drank alcohol in the past month. That may seem like a lot, but it means that 69% didn't drink alcohol in the past month. You're not alone if you choose to not drink.

Myth: "My parents drink, so I should be able to drink, too."

Truth: Parents are not breaking the law when they drink, because they are older than 21. In addition to that, the adult human body and brain handle alcohol differently than the growing teen body and brain.

Myth: "It's only beer, so I won't get drunk."

Truth: A 12-ounce beer contains the same amount of alcohol as a shot of whisky. Any kind of drink with alcohol in it can make you drunk.

Myth: "If I drink, I only hurt myself."

Truth: Drinking often causes dangerous behavior—such as fighting and drunk driving—that hurts many other people.

Myth: "Drugs are a bigger problem than alcohol."

Truth: Alcohol kills more young people than cocaine, heroin, and every other illegal drug combined. There are 18 million Americans who are addicted to alcohol or have **alcohol abuse** issues. People who start drinking at an early age are more likely to abuse alcohol.

It is found in beer, wine, and "hard liquors" such as whiskey, rum, or vodka. It affects the brain, and therefore affects how people think, feel, and act. Other drugs, such as cocaine, meth, or heroin, affect the brain, too. A person can become very ill and addicted to alcohol, just like he or she can be addicted to street drugs.

Alcohol can affect other organs in the human body, including the liver, stomach, and heart, to name a few. And, as with other drugs, a person can die from drinking a lot of alcohol at once. Drinking too much too fast can cause a person to fall asleep and quit breathing. Drinking too much alcohol is linked to about 75,000 deaths per year.

THE TROUBLE WITH ALCOHOL

Despite its happy image in advertising, alcohol is the cause of a lot of sorrow. According to the National Council on Alcoholism and Drug Dependence, almost 18 million Americans have a problem with alcohol. In addition to health problems, many people who drink too much lose their jobs, their friends, and their families. About 20% of suicide victims are **alcoholics**, and alcohol plays a part in nearly half of all traffic accident deaths in the United States.

Drinking brings even more problems for young people than it does for adults. In 2006, the U.S. government published a report on this subject, titled *Call to Action*. In this report, the government asks Americans to do more to stop alcohol use among the country's 11 million current underage drinkers. The federal government has also made clear that it is important to keep other young people from starting. "Research shows that young people who start drinking before the age of 15 are five times more likely to have alcohol-related problems later in life," said Kenneth Moritsugu, an official in the U.S.

government. "New research also indicates that alcohol may harm the developing adolescent brain."

There has been a large drop in tobacco and illegal drug use among teens in the 2000s, but the same is not true for drinking. Compared to underage smokers and drug users, there is a higher number of underage drinkers in the United States. The 2005 National Survey on Drug Use and Health estimates there are 11 million underage drinkers in the United States, and more than 2 million of them are described as "heavy" drinkers. "Alcohol remains the most heavily abused substance by America's youth," Moritsugu said. "We can no longer ignore what alcohol is doing to our children."

ABSTINENCE TO ABUSE

The best way to avoid all of these problems is to not drink at all. This is called **abstinence**. People younger than 21 must abstain from alcohol, and so must pregnant women (because it can harm their unborn babies) and people taking certain types of medicines. And no one should drive after drinking. Even small amounts of alcohol can affect vision, judgment, coordination, and how long it takes to react to obstacles and other cars in the road.

There are other stages of alcohol use between abstinence and abuse. Not all adults who drink alcohol do it to get drunk. Most adults who drink in **moderation** can usually drink safely. Moderate drinking is one or two drinks a day for men, and one for women. Some scientists even believe that moderate amounts of alcohol may lower the risk of some diseases that affect the heart and blood.

Problems with alcohol start with the reason why a person drinks, in addition to how much and how often he or she drinks. Adults who drink mainly at social gatherings,

This blurry, uneven road is an example of what can be seen through the eyes of a drunk driver on a dark, wet evening.

DIFFERENT DRINKS, SAME RESULT

Many people think that beer is a weaker alcoholic drink, and so drinking beer won't make them drunk. That would make sense if a beer were served in the same small glass as hard alcohol. But it's not: Beer is served in larger amounts, such as in a can or a large glass. And one serving like that contains the same amount of alcohol as a small serving of hard liquor. An order of wine will usually be about 5 ounces (1.5 dl), and a beer is often 12 ounces (.35 l). A shot of hard alcohol, such as whiskey, is usually 1.5 ounces (45 ml).

These all contain the same amounts of alcohol. The only difference is that beer contains more water compared to hard alcohol and wine.

Contrary to what many people believe, a pint of beer actually contains the same amount of alcohol as a shot of hard liquor or a glass of wine.

such as dinners or parties, are called social drinkers. They may drink moderately, or they may follow the behavior of other people at the party, even if they drink too much. If someone drinks heavily over a short time, perhaps five or more drinks in a couple of hours, he or she is **binge drinking**. Binge drinkers drink to get drunk as fast as possible, and it's extremely unhealthy.

Alcohol abuse is a pattern or habit of drinking too much. It results in major problems for the drinker, such as fights or car accidents. When one or more of the following problems happen to a person over a year, he or she is an alcohol abuser:

- Can't perform normal tasks at school, home, or work
- Drinking and driving
- Family relationships and friendships harmed by drinking
- Having alcohol-related legal problems, such as being arrested for driving under the influence of alcohol or for physically hurting someone while drunk

Some people who drink a lot may not show any sign of being drunk. That's because over time they have developed a **tolerance** to alcohol. That means that even though they drink the same amount of alcohol, it affects them less. People may say they "hold their liquor well," but it may really be a sign that they drink too much and have a problem with alcohol.

THE DISEASE OF ALCOHOLISM

Alcohol use can seem confusing: Some adults seem able to drink in moderation with no problems at all, while others lose control of their drinking. People with alcohol problems might know their drinking is causing problems in their lives, but they still can't stop. These people are alcoholics. Their minds and bodies crave alcohol.

Alcoholism is the most serious form of alcohol abuse. It is thought of as a **chronic** disease. This means it lasts for a long time and gets worse over time. There are some people who doubt that alcoholism is a disease, partly because when they think of alcohol they think of having fun. And some people do not have a hard time limiting how much they drink. Because of that, they might not be able to understand why others can't quit. They think it just requires more willpower or stronger morals.

Still, it is not so simple for everyone. There are complicated things that go on in the mind and body of an alcoholic. For one, an alcoholic's body becomes used to having alcohol in it, and so he or she needs to drink more and more just to feel normal. The problem often gets worse if the person starts having health problems caused by drinking so much. Those who do try to quit usually can't do it without help because they can have problems with sleeping, uncontrollable body shaking, and stomach pain and vomiting. They might even have seizures within hours after they stop drinking. Yet, if the alcoholic doesn't stop drinking, he or she may die. In addition to causing liver problems, long-term drinking can damage the pancreas, heart, and brain.

A person who starts drinking alcohol at a young age is more likely to become an alcoholic. The only way to recover from this disease is to stop drinking, but it is usually very difficult. One reason why it is difficult is that many alcoholics claim that they don't have a problem. They often really believe this, despite the clear damage it is doing in their lives and the lives of the people close to them. This way of thinking allows the

REASONS NOT TO DRINK

There are plenty of reasons not to drink. Here are a few to keep in mind:

- Memory loss: Alcohol causes "blackouts," periods of time that a person does not remember.
- It weakens performance in sports: Alcohol slows down your ability to do certain physical skills quickly and accurately.
- It can permanently damage the brain: During adolescence, the brain is especially at risk of damage from alcohol, which can harm the brain's growth and development.
- It makes people act foolishly: Alcohol affects a person's judgment and makes him or her unable to completely control aggressive, dangerous, or mean behavior. While drinking, some people think their behavior is funny. When they sober up, they may find that their behavior was far from laughable.
- It can result in problems at school: Many schools, sports teams, and other school activities have suspension rules for drinking on school grounds.
- It's about more than you: Alcohol has widespread effects on families and society. For example, drunk driving can cause injury to many people beyond the person who was drinking.

alcoholic to keep drinking and to blame other people or situations for the problems that he or she is causing. Still, deep down, the drinker may feel guilty, ashamed, and angry about the problems in his or her relationships or at work. Alcoholics may feel self-hatred. To deal with those feelings, they drink more. Often, no matter how bad things get, the alcoholic keeps on drinking.

A POPULAR DRINK

If alcohol is a dangerous substance, why is it still so popular? There are many reasons, but two stand out.

First, making and selling alcoholic beverages is a big business. Alcoholic beverage companies spend huge amounts of money to persuade people to buy their products. For example, in 2005, companies spent $2 billion on advertising on television, radio, billboards, and in newspapers. In addition, they sponsor things such as sports teams, racecars, and special events. Although company leaders say all of this is meant to target adults, many people under age 21 naturally see and feel the influence of alcohol advertising. This is especially true at sports events.

Another reason for alcohol's popularity: It's part of human culture. People have used alcohol as part of social and religious life since the beginning of civilization. There are some exceptions: In parts of the Muslim world—Saudi Arabia, for example—alcohol is forbidden for religious reasons. In the United States, saloons and taverns were the first businesses to take root on the frontier when Americans began moving westward. Now, alcohol flows not just in bars, but also in the average American household.

2

A Very Old Story

Alcoholic drinks have been around just about as long as human beings. Imagine the person who tasted the first "wine." He probably discovered it by accident after sipping from a container of honey or berries that had been sitting around too long. That person probably noticed that the drink made him feel warm, relaxed, and maybe a little drunk. He decided to try making it again and again.

A process called **fermentation** had occurred. Fermentation is a change caused by tiny yeast acting on certain substances that contain sugar (grain or fruit, for example). Yeast grows wild in nature. These tiny fungi grow on plants and animals and spread through the air and water. Yeast is everywhere and will ferment anything possible. In the alcohol fermentation process,

A fermenting tank is filled with pinot noir grapes at Artesa Winery in California's Napa Valley in October 2007. In the process of fermentation, yeast turns sugar into ethyl alcohol and carbon dioxide.

Bacchus is the Roman god of wine, and he is often shown in art as a figure that helps people enjoy themselves, free from their everyday problems. Italian artist Michelangelo created this marble sculpture of the god in 1497.

yeast change sugar into ethyl alcohol and carbon dioxide. Milk turning sour or bread dough rising are other examples of fermentation.

Historians believe that the first alcohol recipe ever was for making beer. Early beer brewers probably experimented with making alcoholic beverages from a variety of foods. The ancient Egyptians made at least 17 kinds of beer and at least 24 kinds of wine. Beer comes from grains, and wine comes from grapes or other fruit. "Hard" alcohol, such as whiskey, comes from fermented grains or juice that is boiled and made stronger in a process called *distillation*. This process makes hard alcohol more alcoholic and "pure" than beer or wine. Most alcoholic beverages do not contain 100% pure alcohol because drinking that can be deadly.

THE ANCIENT WORLD TO THE NEW WORLD

Over time, alcohol became part of social and religious life. For the ancient Greeks, drinking wine took place during gatherings and political discussions. The Greeks

MAKING A TOAST

Today, when people make a "toast" to someone, they raise their glasses and wish the person good health or praise them on a special occasion, such as a wedding. Then they clink their glasses together. The term toast actually comes from the Roman practice of dropping a piece of burnt bread (toast) into the wine before it was served. The Romans did this to take away the acid taste of the wine.

The custom of "drinking a toast" became very popular in the seventeenth and eighteenth centuries. When a party guest had toasted everyone at the party, it became a custom to toast friends who weren't even there, government officials, or anyone else they could think of in order to make the party and the drinking last longer. It was during this period that the tradition of toastmaster, sort of a party referee, was created. The toastmaster at a party made sure that everyone got a chance to offer an equal number of toasts.

mainly drank moderately. The Romans, on the other hand, were known for gatherings that turned into drunken parties. The Roman god Bacchus was the god of wine and is shown in ancient artwork as a wild partier. Bacchanalia, the Roman festivals for Bacchus, were celebrated with dancing, song, and parties. These celebrations got so out of hand that they were forbidden by the Roman Senate in 186 B.C. Some historians say that excessive drinking and other types of moral corruption, especially among Roman leaders, were some of the causes of the end of the Roman Empire.

MORE THAN A PARTY DRINK

Alcohol also was used in religious ceremonies aside from the Greek and Roman traditions. The early Christian Church viewed it as a gift from God to be used and enjoyed. The Bible even encouraged alcohol as a way to ease the hardship of daily life in early times. For example, the Book of Proverbs says, "Give strong drink unto him that is ready to perish, and wine unto them that be of heavy hearts. Let him drink, and forget his poverty, and remember his misery no more." However, the Bible also warns against drinking too much. The Book of Proverbs also says, "Wine is a mocker, strong drink a brawler, And whoever is **intoxicated** by it is not wise."

Over time, people began to use alcohol as a medicine, too. Today, people who have an ache or pain have easy access to pain relievers to make them feel better. Aspirin, for example, can usually be found as close as the medicine cabinet. But in ancient times, alcohol was one of the only sources of pain relief.

Alcohol served other important uses in ancient times. Sometimes, drinks such as beer were a substitute for water that was not clean enough to drink. (The situation was a bit different in Asia, where people commonly boiled water, usually for tea. In this way, they made nonalcoholic beverages that were safe to drink.) As civilizations developed throughout history, people began living closer together in cities and villages. There were no such things as toilets or garbage collectors in early times, so people just dumped their sewage and garbage out in the open. This polluted drinking wells, and the dirty water carried diseases. Alcohol kills germs, so mixing it into contaminated water may have made it a bit safer to drink. People often drank alcoholic beverages to relieve their thirst, rather than to get intoxicated. Alcoholic beverages may have been lifesavers for people who lived without a source of clean water. To this day, this still happens in some poorer parts of the world. Alcoholic drinks have also been an easy source of calories, especially in times when food was in short supply.

ALCOHOL IN AMERICA

Alcohol was an important part of life in the United States from the time of the first colonial settlements. It was popular in the New World for the same reason as in Europe and elsewhere: to celebrate special occasions, for medicine, to feel warmer during the winter, and to forget about bad times. Alcohol was a symbol of people coming together.

Early American settlers used it to honor personal achievements and seal agreements. They used it in religious rituals and to celebrate holidays. Early Americans lacked the beverages that are common today. The water was sometimes polluted. Milk was in short supply and spoiled quickly. Coffee and tea were too expensive. So, drinks such as beer were the perfect alternative.

ALCOHOL'S TERRIBLE EFFECT ON NATIVE AMERICANS

Evidence shows that some Native Americans in what is now the United States made alcoholic drinks before European explorers and settlers arrived in the New World, but it was not a significant part of their culture. Yet, like many other parts of the Europeans' culture, alcohol changed the Native American existence and way of life.

White settlers took advantage of the intoxicating effect on the Native Americans, who had little experience with drinking distilled liquor such as whiskey. The settlers found that if they held meetings about things such as trading and treaties, and made alcohol available at the gatherings, they came away with a much better deal than the Native Americans. Before long, the U.S. government pushed Native Americans onto small pieces of land called reservations. They began to lose their old and proud culture. Though alcohol was not the only cause of the falling culture, it certainly played a big part in the process. With disease, poverty, and few ways to make a living on the reservations, many Native Americans turned to alcohol to alleviate boredom and numb their sadness. The effects of alcohol continue in today's Native American societies and everyday life.

Native Americans today sometimes look to their old traditions to fight against the trap of alcohol abuse. For example, in the Oneida Territory near Syracuse, New York, kids in a new generation of Native Americans are getting in

(continues on page 30)

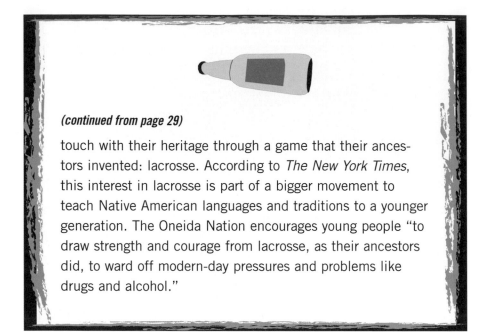

(continued from page 29)

touch with their heritage through a game that their ancestors invented: lacrosse. According to *The New York Times*, this interest in lacrosse is part of a bigger movement to teach Native American languages and traditions to a younger generation. The Oneida Nation encourages young people "to draw strength and courage from lacrosse, as their ancestors did, to ward off modern-day pressures and problems like drugs and alcohol."

TEMPERANCE AND TEETOTALERS

Somewhere between 1790 and 1830, alcohol became a problem for many more people in the United States. In city taverns and saloons in the West, men packed in to drink, gamble, swear, and fight. They spent their wages on drinks and left their families with little money for needs like food, clothing, and shelter.

Then came groups who decided to change all of that. Organizations such as the Women's Christian Temperance Union and the Anti-Saloon League of America were part of the **temperance movement**. These groups were mostly made up of women. They formed temperance "lodges," or clubs, as an alternative to saloons. In these clubs, they offered friendship, community, and a sense of belonging—without the alcohol. People who abstained totally from alcohol were known as "teetotalers."

The Women's Christian Temperance Union was at the forefront of the Prohibition movement in the late 1800s, and the organization is still operating today as a group that promotes abstinence from alcohol. Here, members of the union pack into a bar in 1947 to protest alcohol consumption while the customers remain unresponsive.

PROHIBITION

Temperance groups wanted to ban alcohol completely. That idea gained a lot of support. In 1920, the Eighteenth Amendment to the Constitution, also known as the Volstead Act, went into effect. The law was called **Prohibition**, and it prohibited, or banned, the making, transportation, and sale of any kind of alcohol in the United States.

Prohibition lasted 13 years, from 1920 to 1933. It ended, however, because the law had the opposite effect of what the temperance supporters wanted. Americans believed the right to drink was one of their basic freedoms. Because of this, they found endless ways to get alcohol. They made their own "bathtub gin," and drank in illegal bars called "speakeasies." Prohibition also led to the growth of powerful groups of criminals—

CARRY A. NATION

Carry A. Nation is probably the most famous member of the temperance movement. Her first husband was an alcoholic who drank himself to death. She later married a lawyer named David Nation and settled in Kansas.

Famous for tearing up saloons and liquor stores with a hatchet, Carry A. Nation of the temperance movement shows that she is ready to speak out against alcohol with a Bible in one hand and a hatchet in the other in this image from the early 1900s.

gangsters—who made money from the illegal production and sale of alcohol. Doing this was called "bootlegging." By the end of the 1920s, even the supporters of Prohibition saw that it was a failure. In 1933, the Twenty-first Amendment put an end to Prohibition.

While living there, she organized the local chapter of the Women's Christian Temperance Union—and declared war on alcohol.

Nation was nearly 6 feet tall and weighed 180 pounds. She felt that God himself had called on her to promote temperance with force. She began a campaign of smashing up saloons and liquor stores with a hatchet, shouting "Smash, ladies, smash!" Between 1900 and 1910, she was arrested about 30 times after leading her destructive temperance groups in tearing up one bar after another.

The famous professional boxer John L. Sullivan owned a saloon in New York City. In 1901, an article in *The New York Times* reported that Sullivan had heard about Carry Nation smashing Kansas saloons and said that "if she ever came to his place in New York, he would thrust her into a sewer hole or something." Sullivan, however, wasn't such a tough guy when Nation really did show up outside his saloon. He reportedly ran and hid.

Though the Prohibition era of the 1920s and early 1930s made alcohol illegal, people still managed to get alcohol in many different ways. Some even made it in their bathtubs. On April 27, 1921, officials seized barrels of wine at 38 Cherry Street in New York City.

OTHER WAYS TO CONTROL DRINKING

Since the end of Prohibition, the government has looked for other ways to control drinking in the United States. This includes a special license for selling alcohol. The license means that people can only buy alcohol at certain places, where the store's owner has a license. National, state, county, and city governments each control the sale of alcohol. Because of that, the rules often vary from place to place. Each community has rules about the hours when bars and restaurants may serve alcohol. In addition, there are now tough penalties for drunk driving.

People have argued for many years about whether there should be a minimum age for drinking. Over the

WHAT OTHER COUNTRIES DO

The United States has some of the strictest laws to control drinking in the world. Yet, people in many other countries have different attitudes toward alcohol, and their laws about drinking reflect that.

Many Muslim people refrain from drinking alcohol because it is against their religion, but the actual drinking laws in countries that are primarily Muslim vary. For example, in Saudi Arabia, the sale of alcohol is prohibited. In other Muslim countries, non-Muslims may purchase alcohol. Generally, around the world the most common age to legally purchase or drink alcohol is 18. Yet, some countries have no

The Indonesian government raids unlicensed liquor stores before each celebration of Ramadan, the holiest month in the Muslim calendar. They then destroy the bottles for all citizens to see. Here, the police use road rollers to destroy the seized alcohol in the capital city of Jakarta in 2006.

(continues on page 36)

(continued from page 35)

laws at all that regulate the minimum legal age to drink or buy alcohol.

In many European countries, drinking is not a big issue. Many people there view alcohol as neither evil nor wonderful. The rules about teen drinking are less strict. Countries such as France, Spain, and Germany allow public drinking at ages as young as 16. Many European parents teach their children little by little about how to drink and how not to drink. In France, parents may add a bit of wine to a child's water glass with meals. According to Dwight B. Heath of Brown University, the child's glass has more wine than water by the time he or she is a teenager. Heath argues that this can be a good thing, because it teaches moderation: "There is no mystique [mystery], then, about drinking, and no unrealistic expectation that it will make anyone more good looking, more powerful, or more sexy."

years, each U.S. state has decided its own drinking age. Until 1984, states raised or lowered their drinking age depending on what the public opinion was. For example, during the Vietnam War in the 1960s and 1970s, 18-year-olds were sent to fight abroad. People thought that if a man was old enough to fight in a war, he was old enough to drink. Then, due to a rise in alcohol-related car accidents and deaths, the U.S. government passed the National Minimum Drinking Age Act. This act required all states to only allow people to buy and

U.S. President Ronald Reagan signs legislation at the White House Rose Garden on July 17, 1984 that would require all states to only allow people 21 and older to buy and possess alcohol. He is joined by (*from left*) Transportation Secretary Elizabeth Dole; Rep. John Edward Porter of Ill.; Mothers Against Drunk Drivers founder Candy Lightner; Rep. Gene Snyder of Ky.; New Jersey Governor Thomas Kean; Sen. John Danforth of Mo.; and Sen. Frank Lautenberg of NJ (others are unidentified).

possess alcohol if they were 21 or older. States that did not go along with this would be punished.

The title of the law is confusing, though, because there isn't really a "national legal drinking age." The National Minimum Age Drinking Act doesn't ban drinking under the age of 21. It just bans people under that age from buying and possessing alcoholic beverages.

Today, experts argue about whether the National Minimum Drinking Age law works. The United States has the strictest youth drinking laws in the Western world. At the same time, it has the most drinking-related problems among its youth. There seems to be a connection between these two facts. Most people believe that raising the "drinking age" back to 21 from 18 has helped decrease the number of deaths of young people in traffic accidents simply because, with a higher legal drinking age, fewer teens drink and drive. However, others believe that, while there may be fewer teens drinking and driving, the law has led to an increase in underage binge drinking, especially at colleges and universities. "Just like during national Prohibition, the law has pushed and forced underage drinking and youthful drinking underground, where we have no control over it," said David J. Hanson, an alcohol law expert at the State University of New York at Potsdam.

There are people who agree with Hanson, including John M. McCardell Jr., the former president of Middlebury College in Vermont. He has formed an organization called Choose Responsibility and argues for lowering the drinking age. He also calls for a program to give out licenses for drinking, similar to driver training and licensing. The National Youth Rights Association also calls for lowering the drinking age. The organization calls the minimum drinking age law "the Youth Prohibitionist movement." They argue:

> A lowered drinking age together with greater acceptance of moderate amounts of drinking for younger people will reduce the "forbidden fruit" phenomena. Rather than teach young people about the many uses and abuses of alcohol, current law and policy dictates that alcohol is an inherently evil substance and only total abstinence from alcohol can be preached. While abstinence from alcohol is a totally acceptable option, it should never eliminate the need for honest,

open discussion and education about drinking. Just like any activity in life, drinking responsibly is an activity that one must learn. Currently we deny this healthy process to millions of young Americans. Rather than a gradual introduction to drinking over the period of several years, the current attitude towards youth drinking says that a person shouldn't have a drop of alcohol until their 21st birthday, and at that time it is perfectly fine to consume 21 shots of hard liquor. This is like preventing someone from learning to drive and then handing them the keys on their 16th birthday with instructions to "have fun."

Many others, including Mothers Against Drunk Driving (MADD), oppose lowering the drinking age. Other opponents are the Center for Science in the Public Interest and many branches of national and state government. The struggle to control alcohol use will probably continue for a long time. "In a society that values individual freedom, drawing the lines between rights and responsibilities is hard," says author Lisa Wolff in her book, *Issues in Alcohol*. "Lawmakers must balance the public desire to make their own personal decisions about drinking with their demand to be protected against those who abuse this right. The debate that led to the failed experiment of Prohibition promises to continue into the twenty-first century."

3

Why People Use Alcohol

Students sit through countless lectures warning them about the dangers of alcohol. Many school sports teams require players to sign a form that says the team won't tolerate drinking and if they do they will be penalized. Schools have "zero tolerance" policies stating that students will be punished or expelled for drinking. Students sign "prom pledges," promising not to drink on prom night. Yet, at some point, the warnings seem to lose their effect and alcohol grows in appeal.

ALCOHOL IN THE MEDIA

As discussed previously, the United States has a long history of alcohol use. Alcohol seems to be everywhere. Of course, not everyone drinks, but judging from what

The movie poster for the 1980 film, *Urban Cowboy*—which includes its star, John Travolta—is a prime example of how Hollywood movies use alcohol to attract viewers and give their characters a certain image. Together, the star's name and the movie title have been designed to look similar to a Jack Daniel's liquor bottle logo, and the image of Travolta's cowboy with a beer was created to give viewers the idea that the character is tough and street-smart.

is shown on television, movies, music videos, and the Internet, it may *seem* like they do.

Before turning 18, the average person will see thousands of drinking scenes on television and in the movies. That's in addition to the drinking scenes they see in advertisements. Companies that make and sell alcohol advertise their products in places such as television and radio shows, magazines, and newspapers. They do this to get more people to buy their products.

According to psychologist Henry Wechsler, the alcoholic beverage business is huge—worth about $110 billion per year. It pours about $5 billion into advertising. The problem is that advertising—on television, for example—isn't just limited to people of legal drinking age. "Young male sports fans are the beer industry's biggest customers," Wechsler writes in his book, *Dying to Drink*. "The greatest advertising platform in the world, the Super Bowl, is watched by as many as thirty-three million underage viewers." Young people also see alcohol advertising on the Internet, with company sites featuring games, cartoon characters, and products to buy. Advertising like this may be appealing to young people because it features celebrities and animal mascots such as frogs, lizards, dogs, and horses.

Alcoholic beverage businesses also pay for alcohol education ads that urge people to "drink responsibly." Yet, even those ads may work in favor of the businesses. According to Wechsler, the alcoholic beverage industry actually promotes its products among students through its alcohol education efforts and the campus organizations that it supports. So, he says, while supposedly doing a good deed with their alcohol education messages, the companies are gaining more recognition through advertising.

Researchers have not found a clear answer to whether these positive views of alcohol actually lead to underage drinking. The National Institute on Alcohol Abuse and Alcoholism (NIAAA) reported the results of a study of third, sixth, and ninth graders. Those students who liked alcohol ads were more likely to think drinking wasn't so bad. They were also more likely to want to buy products with alcohol company logos. This study suggests that advertising makes drinking seem like a positive activity.

ONLY THE GOOD SIDE

It's true that alcohol companies make ads that show the positive side of alcohol. But drinking often appears in television shows, too. According to NIAAA, drinking usually appears on television as a background activity. That means characters drink or talk about drinking while doing other activities. There is often no direct message for or against alcohol. According to researchers, drinking is usually presented as a regular activity that doesn't cause problems. Those who drink on television are more likely to be main characters, more attractive, and more popular than those who do not drink on the show. References to the negative results of drinking are rare. This attitude is present on comedy shows, too, when they show "the drunk" as a funny, lovable character rather than a person with a drinking problem.

PEER POWER

Young people receive a dangerous personal message from people around them. The message is that it's okay to drink. People who are the same age, such as classmates in school, are called **peers**. *Peer pressure* is when people try to influence how their peers act, or try to get their peers to do something.

Peers can have both a positive and a negative influence. Teens observe what their peers are doing and learn from it. They often don't realize that they're watching and learning all the time. Maybe a student asks another to join a school club, helps someone with math homework, or shares a great book or a joke. These are examples of behavior that has a happy, positive effect on the

Negative peer pressure can cause a person to do something dangerous or hurtful. It is also one of the strongest forces drawing teens to
alcohol. In an example of overcoming peer pressure, the boy on the left
simply declines an offer of a beer from one of his friends.

other person and others around him or her. Another
example is when someone pressures a bully to quit pick-
ing on another kid.

On the other hand, peers may try to get their friends
to do things they know are wrong. It could be pressure
to skip school or be mean to someone in the group.
They may also pressure their friends to start drinking.
Negative peer pressure is the kind of peer pressure that
causes a person to do something dangerous or hurtful.
It's something everyone has to deal with—even adults.

Peer pressure is one of the strongest forces attract-
ing teens to alcohol. Some teenagers believe that their
friendships are more important than their relationships
with their parents. They want to be liked and to fit in

with their peers. As a result, many young people cannot resist the pressure from peers to join them in drinking. "Peer pressure is huge," says health teacher Matt Nilsen of Edina High School in Edina, Minnesota. "But it's not the media-portrayed peer pressure where one kid tells another, 'If you don't drink this, you aren't cool.' Who says that? But rather, if that guy is drinking and that guy is drinking, what will people think if I am not drinking? . . . Kids don't want to stand out as different, and [they think] 'If I'm not drinking, I'm different.'"

Young people drink for lots of reasons, says Nilsen. Sometimes it is because of depression and wanting to fit in. Some kids give in to peer pressure because they worry that others will make fun of them if they don't go along with the group. Others may go along because they are curious to try something new that their peers are doing. The idea that "everyone's doing it" may influence some teens to leave behind their better judgment or common sense. Adolescence is the time when teens want to grow up quickly, find more independence, and "try out" adult things. Sometimes young people drink simply to rebel or feel older, Nilsen explains. "What does every middle school kid want to be? A high school kid. What does every high school kid want to be? A college kid," he says. But drinking does not make a teenager older. It just makes him or her a young person who illegally drinks alcohol.

Young people sometimes decide to try alcohol as a way to rebel against their parents or other authorities. They may think they can show their anger or "get back" at their parents by doing something parents say not to do. Acting out against the rules offers some excitement. If others in a young person's circle of friends are doing the same thing, the pressure and excitement can be even greater. Teens in particular are drawn to doing reckless things to feel excitement. Researchers now know that there is a physical reason for that. The human brain keeps developing well into a person's twenties. That developing brain may not be able to see ahead to the consequences of dangerous behavior such as drinking.

ADULT ROLE MODELS: GOOD AND BAD

Young people watch the adults in their lives, too. They look to adults for ideas about how to handle situations, and they copy adult behavior. Using alcohol is one way young people attempt to "try out" adult behavior. Most adults try to set a good example for the young people in their lives. Still, even these adults may give a bad message, without even realizing it. For example, adults may joke about the effects of heavy drinking, or give the impression that a person is tough if he or she can drink a lot of alcohol. Other parents may think their children's alcohol use is something all teenagers all do, and therefore is no big deal. According to psychologist Neil Bernstein, "Parents' relationships and behavior send powerful messages to their children about how to cope with problems." If parents always avoid difficult issues and send mixed signals about drinking, they may teach their children that it's okay to drink.

Parents pass on more than their attitudes about drinking. Being a child of an alcoholic or having several alcoholic family members places a person at greater risk for alcohol problems. Research shows that the brains of children of alcoholics are slightly different than the brains of other children. Finding these differences could help to warn against later alcohol problems. The children of alcoholics are between 4 and 10 times more likely to become alcoholics themselves, compared to people who have no close relatives with alcoholism. The children of alcoholics are also more likely to begin

drinking at a young age and to develop drinking problems more quickly.

ESCAPE

According to psychologist Neil Bernstein, being a teenager may be a key risk for starting to drink and also for
drinking dangerously. Life, especially for teenagers, is
stressful, says Doug Eischens, a social worker at Edina
High School in Minnesota. "They have huge demands
on their time and energy," Eischens points out. "They
don't get enough sleep, many don't get enough exercise, and they're often striving to do well. They and
their parents have high expectations. Kids are very
tough on themselves." It is normal for young people to
feel shy about making new friends, or to feel awkward
in social settings. Unfortunately, this can lead some
teens to drink in order to feel more confident and
popular.

Alcohol serves another unhealthy purpose for some
teenagers. When some teens encounter stress in life,
they use alcohol to try to escape. Drinking alcohol may
offer one way to do that, because at first it makes people
feel more relaxed, happy, and self-confident. Eischens
points out that young people often see their parents
having a drink in order to relax. As a result, these young
people might do the same. Their drinking time is the
only relaxing time they have to themselves.

The problems of life don't go away with a bottle of
beer. In fact, because of the things people might do when
they drink too much—such as drunk driving or fighting—drinking can make problems much worse. When
the alcohol wears off, these people may feel ashamed of
their behavior and depressed. Before long, the person
begins to see alcohol as the cure to any unpleasant situation. In many cases, a person will use alcohol as a crutch

STRESS: THE BODY'S ALARM SYSTEM

The human body has developed a reaction to physical danger, often referred to as the fight-or-flight reaction. The body automatically switches into high gear by raising blood pressure and **metabolism**, speeding up breathing, and making the heart beat faster. "It's easy to imagine how this reaction helps you deal with a physical threat," according to the Web site of the Mayo Clinic, a respected medical center in Rochester, Minnesota. "You need the energy, speed, concentration, and agility either to protect yourself or to run as fast as possible."

The fight-or-flight response is set off by psychological or emotional threats, too. This includes being bullied, getting caught in family conflicts, and facing difficult schoolwork and a schedule that's too busy. A person will feel more stressed as he or she faces more stressful events and uncertainty. Even normal day-to-day demands of living can contribute to the body's stress response.

Instead of using alcohol to escape from stress, it's much better to figure out what is causing the feeling of pressure and anxiety. For example, if a person is stressed about a packed schedule, a healthy way of dealing with that might be to stop doing one or two extracurricular activities that aren't important. If the stress is because of difficult classes, it makes sense to get a tutor or other kinds of help in school. Exercise helps relieve many kinds of stress, and so does talking with friends or other trusted people about the stress. Whatever the case, stress does not end after the teenage years. It's a normal part of life, and if handled well, it can help people learn and grow.

to deal with everyday life. It becomes difficult to feel comfortable in a social setting without alcohol.

Young people who feel bad about themselves are more at risk for alcohol abuse. For those who turn to alcohol, the false comfort it gives them is short-lived. "I drank because I was ashamed, and I was ashamed because I drank," says author William Cope Moyers, remembering his battle with alcoholism and drug abuse for many years, beginning when he was a teen. "Which came first, the drinking or the shame? I'm not sure I will ever know the answer to that question, but at some point 'want' became 'need' and I drank and used not to feel better, but to feel normal."

4

How Alcohol Works
in the Body

Munch on an apple, chew a piece of pizza, or guzzle
a glass of milk. Eating and drinking seems so
simple. Yet, the body actually performs an amazing
combination of actions to digest the food people eat.
The body breaks down most food slowly as it moves
through the stomach and intestines. It does this until
the food is in a form that can be taken into the bloodstream and sent throughout the body. This is not the
case with alcohol.

The body digests alcohol differently because of alcohol's unique characteristics. Alcohol is water-soluble.
That means it's made up of very small particles and
mixes easily with water. As a result, it easily travels
around the body, such as from the bloodstream to the

brain. Because of this, it can affect a large number of organs in the body and the things those organs do.

Unlike other foods and drinks, about 20% of the alcohol in a drink passes through the walls of an empty stomach and can reach the brain within one minute— more slowly if a person's stomach is full of food. The remaining 80% passes from the stomach into the small intestine, where it is rapidly taken into the blood and sent throughout the body. It is carried so quickly and to all corners of the body. Because of this, even small amounts of alcohol can affect the body in major ways.

The speed of this whole process depends upon several things:

- The kind of alcohol. For example, an ounce (30 ml) of whiskey contains more alcohol than an ounce of beer. Beverages that contain more alcohol affect the body more quickly than those with less alcohol.
- How the drink is made or mixed. If alcohol is mixed with carbonated beverages such as soft drinks, it can speed up the process.
- What is in the stomach already. Food causes alcohol to be absorbed more slowly.

Other factors that influence how alcohol will affect a person include age, sex, the amount of muscle and fat a person has, and if other drugs are taken along with alcohol.

OUT IT GOES

The stomach and intestines take in alcohol. The liver is what removes it from the body. Alcohol travels through the bloodstream to the liver and every other organ, but the liver is where most of the alcohol is broken down and eliminated from the body. The body releases the waste products of alcohol by exhaling, perspiring, and urinating. Healthy adults break down the alcohol in a standard drink—a 12-ounce beer, for example—in about one hour. Alcohol's effects continue in all parts of the body until the liver can eliminate all of the alcohol.

BLOOD ALCOHOL CONTENT

If a person drinks more alcohol than the liver can handle, the excess alcohol travels around the body until the liver can process it. If a drinker consumes more than one drink per hour, the liver can't keep up. The **blood alcohol content (BAC)** is the amount of alcohol present in the blood. It is measured as a ratio of weight per unit of volume—for example, grams of alcohol per deciliter of blood. Typically this is converted to a percentage. So, for example, a BAC of 0.10% means that that one-tenth of a percent of a person's blood is alcohol. A device called a *breathalyzer* can measure a person's BAC by analyzing the amount of alcohol that is in the person's breath when he or she blows into the breathalyzer.

The BAC rises depending on how much and how fast a person consumes alcohol. Most adults can tolerate one drink during a one-hour period with little change in their ability to function. Still, if a person drinks that one drink much faster—for example, in 10 minutes—the blood alcohol concentration will jump. This leads to less ability to behave and think normally.

In low concentrations, alcohol can make people feel good and more confident. Yet, as the BAC increases, a person's speech becomes unclear, and he or she becomes unsteady and has trouble walking. He or she will also have trouble making good judgments about safety, such

California Highway Patrol officer Mike Robinson (*left*) administers a breathalyzer test to man at a sobriety checkpoint in San Francisco on Dec. 26, 2004.

as whether to get into a car with a drunk driver. With a very high blood alcohol concentration—a BAC of greater than 0.35, for example—a person can die. Many people think that drinking coffee, taking a cold shower, eating bread, or walking outside in cold, fresh air will help a person become sober, but these myths are not true. The only thing that lowers blood alcohol content is time—enough time for the body to process all of the alcohol. Of course, a person can drink much faster than the body can metabolize the alcohol. So, the only thing a person who has had too much to drink can do is to stop drinking and wait until the liver processes the alcohol and the BAC comes down.

EFFECTS OF ALCOHOL ON THE NERVOUS SYSTEM

The nervous system is made up of the brain, spinal cord, and nerves. Nerves are like tiny roads where messages of touch and feeling travel between all the parts

AS THE BAC RISES

The effects of alcohol differ with each person—the person's size, whether the person is male or female, how much he or she has eaten, tolerance for alcohol—but the following is more or less what happens at each BAC level.

In low doses (between 0.02–0.09), alcohol:

- produces a relaxing effect
- lessens shyness and sense of caution
- affects concentration and memory
- slows reflexes and reaction time (how quickly a person can respond to things such as obstacles in the road while driving, an animal running out in the street, etc.)
- reduces coordination

In medium doses (from 0.1 to 0.15), alcohol produces:

- slurred speech
- drowsiness
- changes in emotions and judgment
- greater reduction in balance, vision, reaction time, and hearing

of the body and the brain. Once alcohol is flowing in the blood, it works on the nervous system, particularly the brain. Usually, alcohol has a quieting effect on the brain's activity. Each part of the brain performs different

In high doses (from 0.16 to 0.40 and higher), alcohol produces:

- vomiting
- breathing difficulties
- unconsciousness
- coma
- death

Many people think it's good to let a drunk person simply fall asleep. That way, the person will stop drinking and have time for his or her body to metabolize the alcohol. This thinking is false and extremely dangerous because the person may have drunk so much that he or she has alcohol poisoning. Because there is often still alcohol in the stomach and intestines, alcohol continues to travel around the body whether or not the person is conscious. This means a person's BAC may continue to rise to fatal levels, even if he or she falls asleep and is no longer drinking. This is the time to call 911, not leave the person to "sleep it off." And, the person may not really be sleeping; they may have passed out.

tasks. Alcohol strongly affects the part of the brain called the cerebral cortex. This area processes information from the five senses, comes up with thoughts, and makes decisions. When alcohol works in the cerebral cortex, a person becomes more talkative, more self-confident, and less shy. Soon, though, the person will have trouble processing senses such as vision and hearing, and he or she won't be able to think clearly.

Another part of the brain that alcohol affects is the amygdala. This is the part of the brain that handles emotion and memory. The person can become very emotional, angry, and forgetful when alcohol reaches this part of his or her brain. Another area of the brain, the cerebellum, handles balance and the movement of muscles. People who are intoxicated become less coordinated. For example, they might have trouble walking in a straight line and may lose their balance and fall down.

Many of the actions above—walking, for example— are *voluntary* activities. This means that the person must decide to do them. They don't happen automatically. The brain stem—the very bottom part of the brain— controls *involuntary* activities. This is everything that the body does without the person thinking about it: breathing and heartbeat, for example. As alcohol starts to work on this part of the brain, a person will start to feel sleepy and may eventually fall unconscious.

It becomes extremely serious if the BAC gets high enough to affect breathing, body temperature, and how fast the heart beats. A person will breathe slowly or stop breathing altogether, and both blood pressure and body temperature will fall. These conditions can be fatal. When alcohol affects involuntary actions such as breathing and the gag reflex (which prevents choking), it's easy to see how alcohol can be deadly.

Alcohol has a long-term impact on the brain, too. Scientists still have much to learn about the brain and how it works. Current research shows that heavy drinking damages and shrinks parts of the brain. The result is that those parts of the brain may not function the way they ordinarily would, which influences the person's ability to solve problems or make decisions, among other things. It can also change the individual's personality. The end result can be similar to the way a person's brain may be injured in an accident, such as a severe concussion.

ALCOHOL'S EFFECTS IN OTHER AREAS OF THE BODY

Alcohol is, in fact, a poison, and it has damaging effects on many of the body's organs. In addition to affecting the brain, alcohol:

ALCOHOL EFFECTS: MEN VS. WOMEN

Alcohol appears to affect women more quickly and with greater strength than it affects men. Women reach higher BACs and become more impaired than men after drinking the same amount of alcohol. This is the case even when a man and a woman weigh the same amount. Women's bodies naturally contain more fat and less water than men's bodies. The amount of water and fat is important because alcohol mixes with body water. Since female bodies contain more fat and less water, alcohol becomes more highly concentrated in a woman's body. Therefore, her BAC becomes higher and the woman will feel the effects of that dose of alcohol sooner than the man will.

- Irritates the linings of the stomach and intestines. Also, because alcohol damages the digestive system, many alcoholics can't absorb important vitamins, such as vitamin B-1. This affects their memory and coordination.
- Increases blood flow to the skin, which can disrupt the way the body controls its temperature.
- Restricts blood flow to muscles. This can lead to muscle aches. It may also cause a problem for athletes whose muscles must recover quickly after heavy exercise or muscle strain.

MY ACHING HEAD

When people drink too much alcohol, they usually feel terrible the next day, with what is called a hangover. It usually consists of a headache, a queasy stomach, and fatigue. Dr. Jason D. Rosenberg, the director of the headache clinic at Johns Hopkins University, told *The New York Times* that most authorities agree that hangovers "seem to be caused by a combination of factors resulting from intoxication by alcohol, including dehydration, dilation of blood vessels around the brain, changes in certain chemical levels in the body, and alteration of the sleep cycle." In addition, some additives and chemicals from the fermentation process can contribute to a hangover headache.

- Permanently hurts the liver's ability to break down fats.

Too much alcohol can have an effect on a person's weight, too. Many people associate drinking beer with a "beer belly," a big concentration of fat on the abdomen. Most experts think that a collection of belly fat doesn't come from the alcohol in the beer. Instead, they believe it comes from the *calories* in beer and other kinds of alcohol. All alcoholic drinks are high in calories. For example, an average bottle of beer has about 150 calories. Drinking several beers adds calories to a person's daily intake, and extra calories are stored as fat.

Dehydration occurs as the body processes alcohol and extra water leaves the body. This is why the drinker's body seems to yell out "Water! I'm parched!" the morning after heavy drinking. That message comes in the form of an extremely dry mouth and a headache. A headache from drinking is caused by dehydration, when the body's organs try to make up for their own water loss by stealing water from the brain. This causes the brain to shrink a little and pull on the connections between it and the skull. This is what causes a painful headache. In addition, the body loses important salts, potassium, and sugars that are necessary for proper nerve and muscle function and energy. That leads to headaches, fatigue, and nausea.

MIXING DRUGS AND ALCOHOL

Drinking alcohol while taking medicine is a combination that is deadlier than alcohol alone. Very strong pain medicines and antianxiety medicines such as Valium and Xanax increase the impact of alcohol. The combination affects alertness and reaction time in particular. Cough and cold medicines that contain allergy drugs will also make a person very sleepy when taken with alcohol. Another common medicine, acetaminophen (Tylenol), shouldn't be mixed with alcohol because it can harm the liver. Certain antibiotics cause a problem, too. When taken with alcohol, some antibiotics can cause nausea, headache, and stomach pain. Alcohol and sleeping pills make an equally bad combination.

Mixing alcohol with illegal drugs such as marijuana or narcotic drugs such as heroin is also extremely dangerous. In these cases, alcohol seems to intensify the effect of the drugs. Thus, smoking marijuana and drinking will rapidly affect concentration and coordination. In combination with narcotic drugs, alcohol slows down the operation of the central nervous system and can, for example, make a person stop breathing.

HOW ADDICTION WORKS

Along with the other physical problems alcohol causes, a person who drinks frequently may become addicted to alcohol. Addiction causes chemical changes in the brain, affecting how a person's brain experiences pleasure and reward. People might start drinking just because it makes them feel good. But over time, they keep drinking just to feel "normal."

Society once viewed alcoholism as a moral problem. People thought that an alcoholic drank too much because he or she was a bad person. Yet, alcoholism can happen to smart, kind people, too. "Few people could imagine that a clean-cut, well-mannered, church-going young man like me might have a serious alcohol problem," writes author William Cope Moyers in his book, *Broken: My Story of Addiction and Redemption*. He continues, "No one is immune to the potential power of drugs and alcohol to cause a good person to do bad things."

Scientists are still studying exactly why some people become alcoholics while others do not. They believe a combination of things happen. For one, the risk for alcoholism seems to pass from parents to children. Research has suggested that the children of alcoholics are four times more likely to become alcoholics themselves. This could be partly because they inherit their parents' traits. It could also be because they witness their parents' alcohol abuse at home on a regular basis. Researchers are working to pinpoint exactly what increases a person's risk of becoming an alcoholic. They hope to use this information to develop new medicines to treat alcoholism.

5

Underage Drinking

The teen years are a busy time for the human body. It's a time of great change as the entire body eases into adulthood. Adolescence is when the body grows in height, gains muscle, and develops certain sex characteristics.

Major changes in the brain happen, too. Scientists once thought that a person's brain was finished forming at the time he or she was born. Experts now know that important brain development takes places during the teen years. The frontal lobe (one of the largest parts of the brain) and many nerve pathways and connections continue to develop until the age of 16. The rest of the brain continues to develop for another four years. For anyone who strives to be a good student, a successful athlete, or just plain healthy, drinking alcohol can seriously weaken this important time of development.

ALCOHOL AND YOUNG BODIES

It's challenging enough to be at the top of your game in school and other activities. Alcohol can make it all much harder. Most people underestimate how even a few drinks can erase the hard work done during middle school and high school.

First, alcohol use interferes with the body's ability to use nutrients from healthy foods and drinks. That slows down muscle growth. In addition, since alcohol causes dehydration, it slows down the body's ability to heal sore muscles or injuries. Alcohol slows the body's production of important substances that control growth

ALCOHOL AND ATHLETIC PERFORMANCE

Doing well at sports can be a source of pride and self-confidence. Athletes work hard to get in shape and build muscles, endurance, and sports skills. Drinking alcohol can destroy all that hard work. Alcohol does the following damage to a young athlete:

- Makes a person dehydrated
- Causes problems with keeping a normal body temperature
- Reduces blood sugar levels, which decreases energy levels
- Slows reaction time and weakens coordination and balance

and muscle development. It also reduces the production of an important source of energy for muscles: adenosine triphosphate, the fuel necessary for muscles to contract.

Alcohol also hurts the quality of sleep that a person gets. If you look at someone who is sleeping, it looks like nothing is going on. But in fact, all sorts of important work takes place while a person sleeps. During sleep, the body is hard at work producing the ammunition to fight infections and sickness. Research has also shown a connection between sleep and the ability to stay at a healthy weight. Sleep gives the heart a much-needed rest, too. In addition, much of a person's memory formation takes place at night.

Teenagers need more sleep than adults—about 8.5 to 9.25 hours per night. Though alcohol can make a person feel sleepy, it actually hurts the quality of sleep that person gets. In other words, he or she may sleep, but it's not a deep sleep. Alcohol causes a person to fall asleep more slowly, and also to wake up sooner. After drinking, a person may awaken from dreams and have trouble returning to sleep. The results of lost sleep show up the next day in fatigue and sleepiness. Lack of sleep among teenagers creates a downward spiral of fatigue, emotional problems, poor decision-making, and risky behavior.

Often, alcohol also hurts a person's intake of healthy nutrients. Although alcohol contains a lot of calories, they are "empty calories." This means those calories offer little or no vitamins, minerals, or other healthy substances. In this way, alcohol is much like chips and other junk food. But unlike chips, alcohol can actually hurt the body's ability to process important nutrients from real food, such as B vitamins, folic acid, and zinc.

THE LIVER

When people think of the damage alcohol does to the body, they often think of the liver first. Almost all alcohol is processed in the liver. The liver is the largest organ in the body and it is critical in keeping the body healthy. In fact, scientists have found that the liver is involved in over 500 crucial activities in the body. It stores vitamins, filters toxins and the body's waste products from the bloodstream, and lets out digestive juices into the small intestine, which helps digests food. The liver also performs other important functions, such as helping blood to clot when you cut your finger. Without a healthy, functioning liver, a person can't survive. Excessive drinking can lead to liver disease, including the diseases hepatitis and cirrhosis of the liver.

ALCOHOL AND THE ADOLESCENT BRAIN

As discussed, alcohol can affect a person's thinking, coordination, and other functions while he or she is drinking. But many people don't realize that alcohol may cause much more permanent damage than a headache the next day. During adolescence, the brain is particularly at risk to damage from alcohol, which can harm the brain's growth and development.

Scientists have made important discoveries in the last few years about the effects of alcohol on the brain. Results of studies on deceased people show that those people who had consumed large amounts of alcohol during life had smaller, lighter, more shrunken brains than nonalcoholic adults of the same age and sex. Scientists also use sophisticated machines to view the brains of living alcoholics. Scientists can actually see the changes alcohol consumption makes to the brain. They can watch the brain in action as a person performs tasks, reacts to the environment, or experiences emotions while under the influence. Researchers can then compare and analyze data recorded before, during, and after a person has consumed alcohol. These kinds of studies reveal a relationship between heavy drinking and physical brain damage.

The brain plays a starring role in addiction. According to the National Institute on Alcohol Abuse and Alcoholism (NIAAA), people who start drinking at an early age are more likely to become alcoholics. One survey showed that 47% of people who began drinking before age 14 became alcohol dependent at some point later in their lives. The survey reported that 9% of those who began drinking at age 21 or older became alcoholics.

BINGE DRINKING

On September 4, 2004, Colorado State University student Samantha Spady attended the school's homecoming football game and then went on to multiple house parties around the campus. Samantha finally ended up at a friend's fraternity house, where she began to drink down vanilla-flavored vodka to cheers of "go, go, go!" During the course of about 11 hours, Samantha is said to have consumed 30 to 40 drinks, including beers and shots of vodka.

When it was time to go home, Samantha couldn't talk or walk, so she was put to bed in a room at the fraternity house to "sleep off" her intoxication. Throughout the night, her blood alcohol content continued to rise and she slipped into a coma. A fraternity member was giving his parents a tour of the house the next morning, and found Samantha's body. The hospital said she had died of alcohol poisoning at 6:00 A.M.

Unfortunately, Samantha's case is not unusual. In fact, death by alcohol is common, especially among

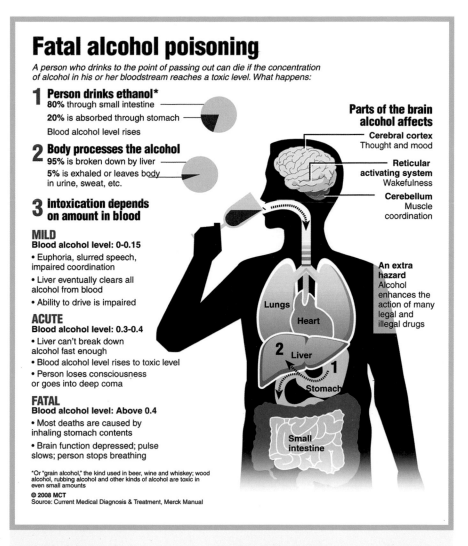

Fatal alcohol poisoning

A person who drinks to the point of passing out can die if the concentration of alcohol in his or her bloodstream reaches a toxic level. What happens:

1 Person drinks ethanol*
80% through small intestine
20% is absorbed through stomach
Blood alcohol level rises

2 Body processes the alcohol
95% is broken down by liver
5% is exhaled or leaves body
in urine, sweat, etc.

**3 Intoxication depends
on amount in blood**

MILD
Blood alcohol level: 0-0.15
• Euphoria, slurred speech,
impaired coordination
• Liver eventually clears all
alcohol from blood
• Ability to drive is impaired

ACUTE
Blood alcohol level: 0.3-0.4
• Liver can't break down
alcohol fast enough
• Blood alcohol level rises to toxic level
• Person loses consciousness
or goes into deep coma

FATAL
Blood alcohol level: Above 0.4
• Most deaths are caused by
inhaling stomach contents
• Brain function depressed; pulse
slows; person stops breathing

**Parts of the brain
alcohol affects**
Cerebral cortex
Thought and mood

**Reticular
activating system**
Wakefulness

Cerebellum
Muscle
coordination

**An extra
hazard**
Alcohol
enhances the
action of many
legal and
illegal drugs

Lungs
Heart
2 Liver
1
Stomach
Small
intestine

*Or "grain alcohol," the kind used in beer, wine and whiskey; wood
alcohol, rubbing alcohol and other kinds of alcohol are toxic in
even small amounts
© 2008 MCT
Source: Current Medical Diagnosis & Treatment, Merck Manual

As this image shows, excessive alcohol consumption can cause death.

college students. Each year, an estimated 1,400 U.S. college students between the ages of 18 and 24 die from alcohol-related incidents, according to the National Institute on Alcohol Abuse and Alcoholism.

Responsible adults do not try to see how fast they can drink alcohol or how drunk they can get. They may have a drink or two at a dinner or social event, but they will stop after that. They know that they must allow their bodies to process the alcohol before their blood alcohol content rises.

For irresponsible drinkers, drinking means one thing only: purposely drinking large amounts of alcohol very quickly in order to get drunk. This is known as binge drinking, and is defined as four drinks for women and

ALCOHOL POISONING: WHAT TO DO

In November 2007, the *Minneapolis Star Tribune* reported the death of one young woman after she drank 21 shots on her twenty-first birthday. "For the rest of their lives, the friends who celebrated her birthday with her that night will wrestle with the guilty questions about whether they could have prevented her death," said one newspaper writer. And it's true that it is possible to prevent the death of someone who has overdosed on alcohol. First, it is important to recognize the signs of alcohol poisoning. They are:

- Vomiting
- Unconsciousness
- Unable to be awakened
- Slow, weak breathing

A person may have one or all of these signs. Acting in time can save a friend's life. Follow these steps if you think you are facing someone who is suffering from alcohol poisoning:

five drinks for men, typically over a four-hour period. When a person binge drinks, as Samantha did, he or she consumes so much alcohol that his or her body can't process it fast enough. When this happens, the BAC rises to a danger point.

Binge drinking in high school, especially among males, often leads to binge drinking in college. Binge drinking is a common cause of alcohol poisoning.

- If you can't wake the person up at all, it is a serious situation. Never let the person just "sleep it off."
- Turn the person on his or her side (to keep him or her from choking in case of vomiting) and do not leave the person alone.
- Check breathing, skin color, and temperature. If the skin is pale, bluish, or cold, or if breathing is irregular (with a few breaths and then nothing for a while), call 911.

Above all, don't hesitate to get help. Some people worry that they or their friend will get in trouble. They might also think that if they call an ambulance, their friend will be mad when he or she wakes up. But action saves lives. The drinker may risk punishment at home, or risk being dropped from a sports team or club. But those consequences are small compared to losing a life.

Teenagers may be particularly at risk for alcohol poisoning because many are first-time drinkers and have never been drunk before. Sometimes their friends or even their own parents leave them to "sleep it off," and they are found dead in the morning.

SOCIAL AND EMOTIONAL CONSEQUENCES

Before long-term physical damage sets in, alcohol poses many short-term dangers. It reduces the ability to make good decisions, makes people do and say things without thinking, and causes some people to behave aggressively. Because of this, people do things while drunk that they would never ordinarily do.

Scientists believe that alcohol abuse and emotional problems go hand-in-hand, especially for young people. For example, according to research by the George Washington University Medical Center, children who abuse alcohol are more likely than their peers to have mental health problems. They are more likely to get into trouble at home, in school, or in the community in general. These young people are:

- Three times more likely to be hospitalized with a mental health problem
- Five times more likely to attempt suicide
- One and a half times more likely to get into an accident, injure, or poison themselves
- Almost twice as likely to have multiple sexual partners

Teenagers who drink have been shown to perform worse in school than their peers who don't drink, according to the American Medical Association. Drinking has been linked with lower grades, poor attendance, and increased dropout rates. Children who are drinking alcohol by seventh grade are more likely to suffer employment problems, abuse other drugs, and commit criminal and violent acts once they reach young adulthood. And they don't necessarily grow out of that behavior as they get older. In fact, the earlier a person starts drinking, the more likely the person is to have problems as they move into adulthood.

The research also shows students who used alcohol by seventh grade are far more likely than nondrinkers to report using other substances. For example, drinkers are far more likely to smoke or use hard drugs. The opposite is true for those who don't drink before age 21.

PAYING THE PRICE

Although they vary, every state has punishments for underage drinking. They range from fines to being required to take alcohol awareness classes to jail time, depending on the situation. Some states take away the driver's license of someone who drives drunk. Most schools have policies against drinking. Many of them have a "zero tolerance" policy, which means that they accept no excuses for the use or possession of alcohol while at school or a school-sponsored event. Punishments may include getting suspended or expelled from school. That, in turn, may mean that students who are caught with alcohol may lose class credits, miss graduating with their class, and may lose college scholarships. If a student is not suspended or expelled, he or she will probably face other punishments. School sports teams and other clubs and activities usually have rules that say a student must sit out several games if he or she drinks. That person may even be kicked off the team for drinking.

The Cost
to Society

Alcohol affects people who drink too much in many ways. It can affect their physical health and even cause death from alcohol poisoning or drinking-related diseases. It can also affect mental health, performance in school, and make people take risks, get in fights, and do other things they would never do ordinarily. But when a person abuses alcohol, it has an impact well beyond that individual. It affects families and society as a whole.

DRUNK DRIVING

One of the most obvious ways one drinker can hurt a lot of people is by drinking and driving. People who drive under the influence of alcohol often cause accidents. They can injure passengers in their own cars, people in

Members of the Maricopa County DUI chain in Phoenix, Arizona, wear bright pink shirts and get ready to perform burials of people who died of alcohol abuse. The men in the chain had been convicted of drunk driving. A spokesman for the sheriff's department said it was the first chain gang to be dedicated to one kind of crime.

other vehicles, and even people just walking down the street.

Drinking and driving is a deadly combination because alcohol hurts coordination, judgment, and reaction time. It wasn't until the 1980s that most people knew just how bad the problem was. "Before the 1980s, drinking and driving was how people got home," said Chuck Hurley, the chief executive officer of Mothers Against Drunk Driving (MADD). Drunk drivers were killing thousands of people each year, but a lot of people didn't realize it because it hadn't happened to anyone

Candy Lightner, founder of Mothers Against Drunk Drivers (MADD), holds a picture in 1981 of her daughter, Cari, who was killed by a repeat drunk driving offender a year earlier. MADD is an international organization that calls attention to the problem of drunk driving, and has been behind the creation of many drunk-driving laws.

they knew. The problem finally got everyone's attention in May 1980 when a drunk driver hit and killed 13-year-old Cari Lightner, who was walking to a church carnival. The impact killed her instantly and literally knocked her out of her shoes. Cari's body landed 125 feet away.

Cari's mother, Candy, and Candy's friend Sue LeBrun-Green did some investigating into the subject of drunk driving. They discovered the size of the problem and found out that drunk drivers usually did not receive very much punishment. They got mad and formed MADD in 1980. MADD chapters sprang up across the country and it became the major organization calling attention to the problem of drunk driving. Over the years, MADD has spread the message all over the country that people should never drink and drive. The group has also been behind the creation of many tough new drunk-driving laws.

Studies show that certain people are more likely to be involved in drunk driving. For example, young men ages 18 to 20 have reported driving while drunk more often than any other age group. There is good news, though. Reports show that fewer young people these days are drinking and driving. Experts think teens now strongly look down on people who drink and drive. Young people have also been using the idea of making someone in their

DRUNK DRIVING IS STILL A PROBLEM

In spite of MADD's work, the problem of drinking and driving has not gone away. MADD calls drunk driving "the most common violent crime." The National Highway Traffic Safety Administration reports these statistics:

- Alcohol-related motor vehicle crashes kill someone every 31 minutes, and every 2 minutes another person is injured but not killed.
- During 2005, 16,885 people in the United States died in alcohol-related motor vehicle crashes. This represents 39% of all traffic-related deaths. In 2005, 16% of drivers ages 16 to 20 who died in motor vehicle crashes had been drinking alcohol.
- Of the 1,946 traffic deaths among people 14 years old and younger in 2005, 21% involved alcohol.

group the "designated driver." The person who has this job does not drink when the group goes out, and therefore can safely drive them all home.

ALCOHOL AND CRIME

Alcohol and crime go hand in hand. In her book, *Issues in Alcohol*, author Lisa Wolff writes, "Each year many thousands of people commit serious crimes under the influence of alcohol, including murder, rape, and robbery. Some claim they don't even remember the act, that they were in a blackout at the time. . . . Studies show

DRINKING AND BOATING

Driving a boat under the influence is just as dangerous as driving a car. The U.S. Coast Guard has found that 23% of boating deaths and 9% of non-fatal boating injuries resulted from accidents in which alcohol or drug use was involved.

On the water, the effect of alcohol is made stronger by the motion and vibration of the boat, engine noise, sun, wind, and water spray, the Coast Guard says. Because of this, a person's blood alcohol content might be low, but it will have worse effects than if he or she were drinking on land. It's illegal to operate a boat—whether a rowboat or the largest ship—under the influence of alcohol. Punishments can include large fines, losing the privilege of driving a boat, and even jail terms.

that, in the United States, 50% to 60% of physical attacks in the home involve alcohol use. One-third to one-half of all batterers are reported to be problem drinkers." About 70% of alcohol-related violent acts happen in people's homes, most often after 11 P.M. Of these acts, 20% involve some kind of weapon.

It's easy to think that alcohol *causes* crime and abuse. But, in fact, many researchers think that alcohol does not cause a person to be violent. Instead, they believe that people who are already abusive are more likely to use alcohol and other drugs. In addition, researchers

Seattle Police Officer Jeff Kappel and Sgt. Dave Proudfoot talk to some boaters during a routine patrol ride on Lake Washington in August 2007.

In an effort to make students realize the horrors of what can happen while driving drunk, many schools stage drunk driving accidents for students to view. Above is a scene from a staged accident at Dunsmuir High School in California.

believe that alcohol reduces the voices in a person's head that normally keep his or her aggressive behavior under control. In other words, it shuts off the little voice that says, "You can't do that."

The problem is worse for anyone who starts drinking at an early age. A study at Boston University found that teen who started drinking at a young age are more likely to be involved in alcohol-related violence as adults. The research revealed that those who started drinking before age 17 were 3 to 4 times more likely to have been in an alcohol-caused fight at some time in their lives, compared to adults who began drinking after age 21. Also, young people who have alcohol problems are 4.5 times more likely to get into a serious fight and 3.5 times more likely to carry a weapon.

ALCOHOL AND FAMILIES

When parents abuse alcohol, their children suffer. Children with a parent or caregiver who abuses alcohol often grow up with a number of problems as a result. Statistics suggest that alcohol plays a part in about one-quarter of known cases of child abuse.

Alcoholic parents are three times more likely to abuse their children and four times more likely to neglect them than parents who do not abuse alcohol. Children of alcohol abusers face a greater risk of accident and injury, as well as a greater risk of failure in school. They are more likely to suffer from behavior disorders, depression, or anxiety. Those conditions then increase the chance that these children will smoke, drink, or use drugs. Then, one generation's problem continues on with the next generation. Almost one-quarter of American youth live in a home where at least one parent or other adult is a binge drinker or heavy drinker.

Even if they aren't abused, the children of alcoholics often grow up in difficult situations with a lot of conflict and arguing. The parent who drinks can be unpredictable, and may fail to comfort and support his or her children. As a result, children in this situation often have trouble trusting other people, and have problems making lasting friendships. They may fear that their parents or others will abandon them.

Families often avoid talking about their alcohol problems. It's a difficult subject to discuss. Family members, even children, may try to cover up the problem and take over many of the jobs that the alcoholic parent should be doing. That's one reason alcoholism is often called a "family disease." To keep family life functioning,

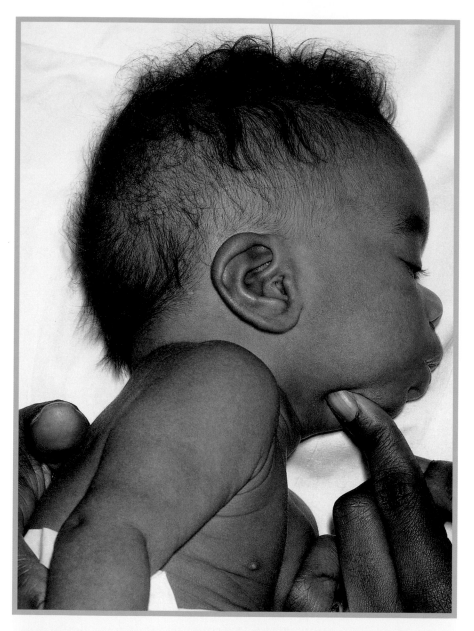

This fragile four-month-old baby was born with fetal alcohol syndrome, which occurs when a mother drinks too much alcohol during pregnancy. Alcohol in a pregnant woman's bloodstream interferes with the fetus's ability to receive adequate oxygen and nourishment. This can result in several birth defects.

children of alcoholics commonly "grow up too fast," meaning that they take on big responsibilities such as housekeeping, bill-paying, and cooking. In their book, *Working with Children of Alcoholics*, family development experts Bryan E. Robinson and J. Lyn Rhoden call these children family heroes. "Family heroes," they say, "are ten years old going on thirty-five and are determined to prove to the world that everything is normal at home."

THE YOUNGEST VICTIMS

Drinking can have tragic effects on children even before they are born. If a woman drinks too much while she is pregnant, the alcohol interferes with the baby's development. The result is a condition called **fetal alcohol syndrome**. Children born with fetal alcohol syndrome have a variety of physical and mental problems including poor growth, physical deformities, low intelligence, and learning disabilities. The syndrome is completely preventable if a pregnant woman abstains from alcohol. Even so, 40,000 infants are affected each year, according to the National Organization on Fetal Alcohol Syndrome. Drinking during pregnancy is the leading cause of preventable mental retardation and birth defects in the United States.

THE FINANCIAL COST

The problem of alcohol abuse and alcoholism also brings a huge financial cost to families and society. For example, a person with fetal alcohol syndrome needs more than $800,000 for special medical care during the course of his or her lifetime. In 2003, $5.4 billion was spent to treat fetal alcohol syndrome in the United States.

Car accidents and other alcohol-related injuries bring costs, too, for things such as medical care for victims and vehicle repair for crashed cars. In addition to that, alcoholics frequently have health problems such as liver disease, digestive disorders, and heart disease. It's nearly impossible to figure out the total cost, but some people estimate that the price of alcohol abuse and alcoholism is between $7 billion and $10 billion each year. The cost of the problems related to alcohol is huge, and everyone pays.

Prevention
and Treatment

Dealing with alcohol problems can be tricky. Some people may have problems with alcohol and not know it. Others may know but don't want to admit it to themselves or to others. Fortunately, there's a lot of help available for people who would like to quit drinking or who want to learn more about alcohol abuse and alcoholism.

SIGNS OF A PROBLEM WITH ALCOHOL

The first step in solving an alcohol-related problem is for the drinker to admit that he or she *has* a problem. The following questions can help you find out if you, a friend, or a family member has a drinking problem:

- Does the person use alcohol to deal with stress, an argument, or relationship problems?

- Has drinking interfered with the person's ability to go to school or get work done on time? Are the person's grades or job skills slipping?
- Has the person ever had a memory loss from drinking?
- Has he or she ever been injured, injured someone else, or damaged property while drinking?
- Has the person ever felt he or she should cut down on drinking?
- Have people annoyed the person by criticizing him or her for drinking?
- Has the person ever felt bad or guilty about drinking?
- Has he or she ever had a drink first thing in the morning to steady nerves or to get rid of a hangover?
- Does he or she regularly drink with the intention of getting drunk?
- Has he or she ever been arrested for a crime related to alcohol?

A "yes" answer to any of these questions may suggest that the person does have alcohol problems. Anyone who thinks he or she might have a problem should see a doctor or other health professional right away. A health expert can help determine if the person has a drinking problem, and then help plan what to do.

Still, sometimes the person with the drinking problem doesn't realize there is a problem, or won't admit it. In that case, someone else may need to start the discussion. It's often difficult to tell someone that you think he or she has a drinking problem. If it's a friend, you might worry that he or she will get angry and not want to be your friend anymore. Yet, ignoring the problem won't help that person. Here are some things you can do if you see signs of an alcohol problem in a friend or loved one:

- Let the person know that you are worried that drinking is affecting your relationship.
- Be specific about the things you have seen happen while he or she is drinking. Avoid shouting or saying that this person is bad for what he or she does. Stick to the facts.
- Share your concerns in private with another person who is knowledgeable about such problems. This could be a school counselor, member of the clergy, or social worker.
- Don't cover for the person's behavior. You are not responsible.
- Set limits on what you will do with the person if he or she continues to drink. Do not ride with him or her in a car or other vehicle.

BEATING THE BOTTLE

People who are not alcoholics but who have abused alcohol may have an easier time getting better. They might be able to limit the amount they drink, or they could simply decide to quit drinking on their own. However, for people who have a serious problem with alcohol, simply trying to cut down rarely works. They must quit drinking completely and they usually can't do it by themselves.

Quitting alcohol is hard because alcohol causes physical and emotional problems. When a person stops drinking, his or her body reacts with **withdrawal** symptoms. The symptoms include shaking, seizures, and hallucinations ("seeing things"). Going through withdrawal usually requires going to a treatment center. Doctors there can provide medicines to help control the symptoms of withdrawal. Treatment may also include medical checkups and counseling.

Researchers are inventing and studying new medicines to help alcoholics in their battles to recover. One medicine, called disulfiram (Antabuse), discourages drinking by making a person sick if he or she drinks alcohol. It produces a strong physical reaction that includes flushing, nausea, vomiting, and headaches in anyone who drinks. The medicines Naltrexone and Vivitrol reduce the urge to drink, too. Acamprosate (Campral) is a medicine that may help a person by reducing his or her cravings for alcohol.

People with very serious problems might live at a special treatment center for several weeks or months. Many of these centers begin treatment with a program of **detoxification**. This will get the alcohol out of the person's system. It usually takes about four to seven days. The person may need to take medicines to prevent seizures and hallucinations during withdrawal. In a treatment center, experts examine and treat common physical problems related to alcoholism, such as high blood pressure, increased blood sugar, and liver and heart disease.

Patients also receive emotional support and treatment. They will usually talk about their problems with a counselor. Sometimes they do this alone, and sometimes they join a group of other recovering alcoholics. Many treatment programs also offer a kind of therapy in which the alcoholic and his or her family all meet together with the counselor. Family support can be an important part of an alcoholic's recovery.

RELAPSE

Alcoholism treatment works for many people. However, many alcoholics still find it difficult to fight their cravings for alcohol after they have gone through treatment programs and counseling. These people are in danger of **relapse**, which means they go back to drinking. Sometimes a relapse will last just a few days. Sometimes it sends the alcoholic right back to where he or she started. Some people are successful in treatment, and some people are not. Some people stop drinking and remain sober. Others have long periods of being sober but have a relapse every once in a while. There are others who cannot stop drinking for any length of time. One thing, however, is clear: The longer a person abstains from alcohol, the more likely he or she will be able to stay sober.

ALCOHOLICS ANONYMOUS
No one is ever really "cured" from alcoholism. Recovery is a life-long effort. Special programs and support groups can help an alcoholic after he or she finishes medical treatment. Special programs help people recovering from alcoholism or alcohol abuse to abstain from drinking, manage relapses, and cope with necessary lifestyle changes.

Alcoholics Anonymous (A.A.) is the most well known of these groups. A.A. describes itself as "a fellowship of men and women who share their experience, strength, and hope with each other that they may solve their common problem and help others to recover from alcoholism. The only requirement for membership is a desire to stop drinking." The group was founded in 1935. It believes that successful treatment is impossible unless the alcoholic accepts that he or she is addicted. There is no reason to be ashamed as long as the person makes that effort, group members say.

Alcoholics Anonymous estimates that there are more than 100,000 A.A. groups and more than 2 million members in 150 countries. Alcoholics can become involved with A.A. before entering professional treatment, or they can use A.A. as a part of their treatment. They can also decide to join after finishing treatment at a medical center. The organization offers different kinds of

THE 12 STEPS OF ALCOHOLICS ANONYMOUS

Alcoholics Anonymous (A.A.) requires that its members quit drinking. For alcoholics, that's not easy, but by going to regular A.A. meetings, they find support from other A.A. members to avoid drinking. One of the main ideas of A.A. is to do it "one day at a time," instead of thinking about the larger task of not drinking forever.

The organization believes that alcoholics can begin to heal their bodies when they stop drinking, but to stay sober they must also heal the personal and psychological problems of alcoholism—feelings of guilt, for example. A.A. encourages its members to follow the organization's "Twelve Steps" to recovery in order to straighten out "confused feelings and unhappy feelings." The steps are based on the experiences of A.A.'s earliest members and, as you can see, focus a great deal on turning one's life over to God, or some higher power.

1. We admitted we were powerless over alcohol—that our lives had become unmanageable.
2. Came to believe that a power greater than ourselves could restore us to sanity.
3. Made a decision to turn our will and our lives over to the care of God as we understood him.

meetings. For example, "speaker meetings" are open to both alcoholics and nonalcoholics. These meetings offer the best way to learn what A.A. is about. At speaker meetings, A.A. members tell their stories. They describe their

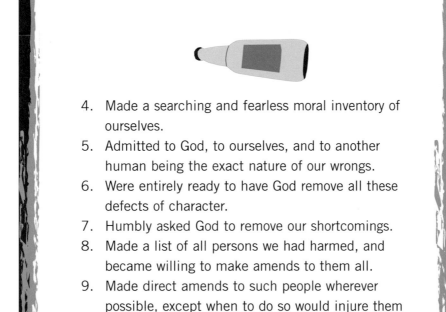

4. Made a searching and fearless moral inventory of ourselves.
5. Admitted to God, to ourselves, and to another human being the exact nature of our wrongs.
6. Were entirely ready to have God remove all these defects of character.
7. Humbly asked God to remove our shortcomings.
8. Made a list of all persons we had harmed, and became willing to make amends to them all.
9. Made direct amends to such people wherever possible, except when to do so would injure them or others.
10. Continued to take personal inventory and when we were wrong promptly admitted it.
11. Sought through prayer and meditation to improve our conscious contact with God, as we understood him, praying only for knowledge of his will for us and the power to carry that out.
12. Having had a spiritual awakening as the result of these steps, we tried to carry this message to alcoholics, and to practice these principles in all our affairs.

SOBER SCHOOLS

For teens recovering from addiction, high school can be a huge challenge. Drugs and alcohol are easy to find in many schools, and so is the pressure to use them. Hanging around with the same friends who still drink or do drugs makes it almost impossible for recovering students to stay clean and sober. Studies show that about 80% of students who return to the same high school after treatment begin using drugs or alcohol again.

A few communities across the country have developed another choice: special high schools designed to support the recovery of young people with substance abuse problems. These schools are often called "dry highs," "sober highs," or "recovery highs." They provide a place where students can work on recovery while they work to earn their high school diplomas.

Recovery schools offer the same kinds of classes as regular high schools. The difference is that all of the students are in recovery, and so staff and fellow students are dedicated to supporting that process. All students are required to be alcohol-free and drug-free. Some schools conduct random drug and alcohol tests, while other schools have students sign a contract saying they will stay sober. Evidence shows that fewer students in these schools experience relapse compared to students who attend traditional schools.

There is more information on recovery high schools and colleges on the Association of Recovery Schools's Web site, www.recoveryschools.org.

experiences with alcohol, how they came to A.A., and how their lives have changed as a result. "Closed meetings" are similar to speaker meetings, but they are only for members or people who are interested in joining.

Not everyone agrees that the A.A. approach is the answer for all alcoholics, but it does work for some people. One reason that A.A. might work is that members often replace their old group of drinking friends with a new group of A.A. friends. These new friends can motivate and support the person to keep abstinent. Also, A.A. teaches skills to deal with the urge to drink, as well as skills to rebuild lives and relationships.

AL-ANON AND ALATEEN

The organizations Al-Anon and Alateen were formed to support the friends and family members of alcoholics. Al-Anon is for family members and friends, and Alateen is especially for teenagers struggling to deal with a loved one's alcohol problems.

These two groups use many of the same ideas that have worked in A.A. Members direct the meetings and they share their own experiences, strengths, and hopes with each other. These organizations offer the chance to meet others who share the feelings and frustrations of life with an alcoholic. Members work to "recover" from the effects of dealing with a loved one's drinking. They hope to learn a better way of life, and to find happiness whether the alcoholic is still drinking or not. Members learn that in order to help a drinker, they must first help themselves.

A.A., Al-Anon, and Alateen are all controversial. There are many scientific studies that support the idea that alcoholism is a disease, but some people don't see it that way. The idea that alcoholism is a lifelong disease is a "myth," according to psychologist Stanton Peele, Ph.D., in his 1989 book, *Diseasing of America*. Peele believes that treating alcoholism like a disease gives drinkers an excuse for their bad behavior. He views alcoholism as a personal conduct problem, and says most people can overcome addiction and their bad behavior on their own.

AVOIDING ADDICTION

The best way to prevent problems with alcohol is to avoid drinking. Avoid the parties and other situations where drinking will take place. Talk to friends or parents ahead of time so you have a plan for what to do if a situation gets out of hand. Plan ways to get home if you find yourself with a driver who is drinking. "Know ahead of time what you want to do when you find yourself in a situation with alcohol, and have strategies ahead of time to cope with drinking situations," says social worker Doug Eischens. "There's no way that you won't have to grapple with this issue at some time." Be ready to turn down alcohol if someone offers it to you. A simple "no, thanks" will do in most cases. It can really help to have at least one friend who is willing to say "no," too. It makes it easier to resist peer pressure. Good friends with values similar to yours will back you up when you don't want to do something.

Think about your values, about what behavior you admire in other people, and about the type of friends you want to have. Being able to deal with peer pressure is a skill that is useful throughout life. Peer pressure doesn't stop when you graduate from high school, turn 21, or move to a new town. Adults, too, must deal with it. And standing up against peer pressure shows maturity much more than drinking does.

It's important to understand the facts about alcohol and how it affects a person physically, mentally, and socially. This understanding will give you the confidence to make the right choices about drinking, no matter what other people are doing. Confidence comes from the inside, not from how much a person drinks, smokes, or takes risks.

Sometimes not drinking can be a lonely choice. Saying "no" may mean drifting away from old friends who prefer people who drink. Inner strength and self-confidence can help you stand firm, walk away, and resist doing something bad when you know better. And don't worry. There are plenty of people out there who are interested in things besides hanging out in someone's basement or out in the woods and drinking beer all night.

POSITIVE PEER PRESSURE

If enough young people get together, they can pressure each other into doing what's right. One example is the Sober Squad at Edina High School in Edina, Minnesota. The group meets every week to discuss alcohol issues in the news and other hot topics. They talk about friends' and families' issues with alcohol, and they support their peers who decide to go to Al-Anon or Alateen.

The group also visits local elementary and middle schools to talk about why kids try alcohol. Members explain the consequences of using alcohol and how to avoid drinking. "The group is made up of people who have tried drinking and think it's stupid, and people who don't drink and don't want to," explains one member of the Sober Squad. "We support each other. It's important not to feel like you're the only one who isn't drinking."

Investigate other social groups such as sports teams and clubs, activities such as theater, and faith-based groups. There are so many interesting groups to explore. Plan a trip to the movies, the mall, a concert, or a sports event. Organize friends to go bowling or get a group together to play Ultimate Frisbee. By choosing not to drink, you're showing leadership, and you're on your way to being a healthy adult.

ALCOHOL CHRONOLOGY

About 10,000 B.C.	Early humans apparently discover fermentation by accident. (Beer jugs from this period have been discovered.)
4200 B.C.	Scenes showing fermentation appear on ancient Mesopotamian pottery. Rules about bars are passed. Sumerians and Egyptians use alcohol in medical treatments.
1700 B.C.	Winemaking becomes common in Greece. Over time, people started using it in daily meals, religious rituals, and medicine.
1116 B.C.	A royal Chinese law announces that heaven approves of the use of alcohol in moderation.
About A.D. 30	Early Christians view wine as a gift from God. Christianity and winemaking skills spread at the same time through Western Europe.
A.D. 100	The first brandy is distilled.
Middle Ages (A.D. 476 to 1500)	Monasteries become centers of winemaking knowledge.
A.D. 625	The Prophet Mohammed tells his followers to abstain from alcohol.
1250	Arnaud de Villeneuve distills wines in France. He calls his product *eau de vie,* or "water of life." He claims that people who drink it will live longer.
1784	Dr. Benjamin Rush identifies alcoholism as a disease.
1791	The U.S. government charges tax on distilled alcohol to raise money to pay off Revolutionary War debts, and to demonstrate the power of the national government.

1794	A group of farmers in Pennsylvania refuses to pay taxes on the whiskey they made. This event is now known as the Whiskey Rebellion.
1880s	The temperance movement begins in the United States.
1920	The Eighteenth Amendment (also known as the Volstead Act) goes into effect.
	Prohibition begins. Breweries make root beer as an alternative to beer.
1933	The Twenty-first Amendment ends Prohibition.
1935	Alcoholic Anonymous is formed.
1951	Al-Anon is formed for people who must deal with friends or family with alcohol problems.
1970 to 1975	The minimum legal drinking age is lowered to 18, 19, or 20 in 29 states.
1980	Mothers Against Drunk Driving is formed.
1984	The National Minimum Drinking Age Act outlaws purchase and public possession of alcohol by those under the age of 21.

GLOSSARY

Abstinence   The practice of staying away from a substance

Alcohol abuse   A pattern of drinking that makes a person unable to perform normal tasks

Alcoholic   A person who cannot stay away from alcohol even though his or her health and quality of life suffers because of it

Binge drinking   The dangerous practice of drinking large amounts of alcohol in a short amount of time. Binge drinking carries a serious risk of alcohol poisoning.

Blood alcohol content (BAC)   The measurement of the amount of alcohol in the bloodstream

Chronic   Occurring often and over a long period of time

Dehydration   Water loss in the body. Sweating or drinking too much alcohol can make a person dehydrated.

Detoxification   A process in which the body is allowed to free itself of a drug

Fermentation   A chemical process by which the sugar in a liquid turns into alcohol and a gas. For example, yeast and certain bacteria cause fermentation in fruit juices.

Fetal alcohol syndrome   A group of physical and mental birth defects caused by a woman drinking during pregnancy

Intoxicated   The condition of being drunk

Metabolism   The process by which living things change food into energy and living tissue, and dispose of waste material

Moderation   Drinking small, controlled amounts of alcohol; not drinking to get drunk

Peers   Equals, or people of the same age or in the same social circle

Prohibition   The period from 1920 to 1933 in the United States when it was illegal to produce, sell, and drink alcohol

Relapse   To fall back into a bad habit after the habit was stopped for a while

Temperance movement   A campaign in the United States that tried to greatly reduce the amount of alcohol people drank. Most people in the temperance movement wanted to make producing, selling, and drinking alcohol completely illegal.

Tolerance   A condition in which a drinker needs more and more alcohol to feel the same as he or she used to feel after drinking smaller amounts

Withdrawal   A process that occurs when a person who is addicted to alcohol stops drinking

BIBLIOGRAPHY

"After losing Amanda, talk about drinking." *Minneapolis Star-Tribune*, November 3, 2007, A14.

Alcohol/Drug Information Center. "Effects of Alcohol Intoxication." Indiana University. Available online. URL: http://www.indiana.edu/~adic/effects.html. Accessed January 16, 2008.

Alcoholics Anonymous. "Information on AA." Available online. URL: http://www.aa.org/en_information_aa.cfm. Accessed January 17, 2008. and http://www.alcoholics-anonymous.org/en_pdfs/p-42_abriefguidetoaa.pdf Accessed February 12, 2008.

American Medical Association. "Brain Damage Risks." Available online. URL: http://www.ama-assn.org/ama/pub/category/9416.html. Accessed January 16, 2008.

Barr, Andrew. *Drink: A Social History of America*. New York: Carroll & Graf Publishers, 1999.

Bernstein, Neil I. "Why Teenagers Use—and Abuse—Alcohol and other Drugs." Partnership for a Drug-Free America. Available online. URL: http://www.drugfree.org/Parent/Knowing/Why_Teenagers_Use_and_Abuse. Accessed January 16, 2008.

BUPA UK. "Alcohol and the Athlete." Available online. URL: http://www.bupa.co.uk/health_information/html/healthy_living/lifestyle/exercise/diet_exercise/athalc.html. Accessed January 20, 2008.

Butler, Katy. "The Grim Neurology of Teenage Drinking." *New York Times*, July 4, 2006. Available online. URL: http://www.nytimes.com/2006/07/04/health/04teen.html. Accessed January 16, 2008.

Center of Alcohol Marketing and Youth. "Alcohol Advertising and Youth." Georgetown University. Available online. URL: http://camy.org/factsheets/index.php?FactsheetID=1. Accessed January 16, 2008.

Choose Responsibility. Available online. URL: www.chooseresponsibility.org. Accessed January 16, 2008.

Eischens, Doug (social worker at Edina High School, Edina, Minnesota). In discussion with author. December 4, 2007.

George Washington University. "Ensuring Solutions to Alcohol Problems." Available online. URL: www. alcoholcostcalculator.org. Accessed January 16, 2008.

Heath, Dwight B. *Drinking Occasions, Comparative Perspectives on Alcohol and Culture.* Philadelphia: Taylor & Francis, 2000.

Hobbs, Thomas R., Ph.D., M.D. "Managing Alcoholism as a Disease." *Physician's News Digest.* Available online. URL: http://physiciansnews.com/commentary/298wp.html. Accessed January 17, 2008.

Hu, Winnie. "Indians Widen Old Outlet in Youth Lacrosse." *The New York Times*, July 13, 2007. Available online. URL: http://www.nytimes.com/2007/07/13/nyregion/13lacrosse. html?_r=1&oref=slogin. Accessed January 17, 2008.

Johnson, Alex. "Debate on lower drinking age bubbling up." MSNBC, August 14, 2007. Available online. URL: http:// www.msnbc.msn.com/id/20249460. Accessed January 17, 2008.

Lawrence, Bruce A., Ted R. Miller, and L. Daniel Maxim. "Recent Research on Recreational Boating Accidents and the Contribution of Boating Under the Influence." U.S. Coast Guard, Boating Safety Division, July 2006. Available online. URL: http://www.uscgboating.org/statistics/BUI_ Study_Final.pdf. Accessed January 17, 2008.

The Marin Institute. "Alcohol and Youth." Available online. URL: www.marininstitute.org/Youth/alcohol_ads.htm and http://www.marininstitute.org/Youth/alcohol_youth.htm Accessed February 13, 2008.

Mayo Clinic Staff. "Stress: Unhealthy response to the pressures of life." MayoClinic.com, September 12, 2006. Available online. URL: http://www.mayoclinic.com/health/ stress/SR00001. Accessed January 17, 2008.

Mothers Against Drunk Driving. Available online. URL: www. madd.org. Accessed January 17, 2008.

"Moyers on Addiction: Close to Home." www.wnet.org/ closetohome/home.html Accessed February 12, 2008.

Moyers, William Cope. *Broken: My Story of Addiction and Redemption.* New York: Penguin Group, 2006.

National Institute on Alcohol Abuse and Alcoholism (NIAAA). Available online. URL: http://pubs.niaaa.nih.gov/ publications/arh283/155–162.pdf . Accessed February 13, 2008.

National Organization on Fetal Alcohol Syndrome. "FASD: What Everyone Should Know." Available online. URL: www.nofas.org/MediaFiles/PDFs/factsheets/everyone.pdf. Accessed January 16, 2008.

New York Times, "Mrs. Nation Paid A Visit To New York" August 29, 1901. Available online: URL: http://query. nytimes.com/gst/abstract.html?res=9B02E3DF1E39EF32A257 5AC2A96E9C946097D6CF

Nilsen, Matt (teacher at Edina High School, Edina Minne- sota). In discussion with author. December 5, 2007.

Pegram, Thomas R. *Battling Demon Rum: The Struggle for a Dry America, 1800–1933.* Chicago: Ivan R. Dee, 1998.

RAND Health. "Study Links Early Alcohol Use and Behavior Problems in Young Adulthood." Boston University School of Public Health, May 2003. Available online. URL: http:// www.jointogether.org/news/research/pressreleases/2003/ study-links-early-alcohol-use.html Accessed February 13, 2008

Robinson, Bryan E. and J. Lyn Rhoden, *Working with Children of Alcoholics.* Thousand Oaks: SAGE Publications, 1998.

State University of New York at Potsdam. "Alcohol Problems and Solutions." Available online. URL: http://www2. potsdam.edu/hansondj. Accessed January 16, 2008.

Steubs, Kelly (student at Edina High School, Edina, Minnesota). In conversation with author. November 17, 2007.

University of Massachusetts. "Facts for Athletes About Alcohol." Available online. URL: http://www.gmu.edu/student/hwc/saps/pdfs/factsathletesaboutalcohol.pdf. January 16, 2008.

Volkmann, Chris and Toren Volkmann. *From Binge to Blackout: A Mother and Son Struggle with Teen Drinking.* New York: New American Library, 2006.

Wagner, Angie. "Danger of Binge Drinking Continues." *Lincoln Journal Star*, November 28, 2004. Available online. URL: http://www.journalstar.com/articles/2004/11/29/local/doc41aa8de30713f284825611.txt. Accessed January 17, 2008.

Watson, Stephanie. "How Alcoholism Works." How Stuff Works. Available online. URL: http://health.howstuffworks.com/alcoholism4.htm. Accessed January 17, 2008.

Williams, Alex, "Hangover Helpers: Beyond Sheep Eyes," The New York Times,

Published: January 1, 2006 URL: http://www.nytimes.com/2006/01/01/fashion/sundaystyles/01HANGOVER.html?scp=1&sq=causes+of+hangover&st=nyt. Accessed February 12, 2008.

Wechsler, Henry and Bernice Wuethrich. *Dying to Drink.* Emmaus, Pa.: Rodale, 2002.

Wolff, Lisa. *Issues in Alcohol.* San Diego: Lucent Books, 1999.

FURTHER READING

Aretha, David. *On the Rocks: Teens and Alcohol*. London: Franklin Watts, 2007.

Cherniss, Hilary, and Sara Jane Sluke. *The Complete Idiot's Guide to Surviving Peer Pressure for Teens*. Indianapolis: Alpha, 2002.

Packer, Alex J., Ph.D., *Wise Highs—How to Thrill, Chill, & Get Away From It All Without Alcohol or Other Drugs*, Free Spirit Publishing, Minneapolis: 2006.

Shannon, Joyce Brennfleck (ed). *Alcohol Information for Teens: Health Tips about Alcohol and Alcoholism*. Detroit: Omnigraphics, 2005.

White, Tom. *Bill W.: A Different Kind of Hero: The Story of Alcoholics Anonymous*. Honesdale, Pa.: Boyds Mills Press, 2003.

WEB SITES

TEENSHEALTH
http://www.kidshealth.org/teen

TeensHealth provides teens and families with accurate, up-to-date health information they can use.

THE COOL SPOT
http://www.thecoolspot.gov

The National Institute on Alcohol Abuse and Alcoholism (NIAAA) gives tips on resisting alcohol and peer pressure.

ALATEEN
http://www.al-anon.org/alateen.html

Alateen helps teen family members and friends of alcoholics recover from the effects of living with their loved ones' problem drinking.

ALCOHOL SCREENING: HOW MUCH IS TOO MUCH?

http://www.alcoholscreening.org

Fill out a questionnaire to determine if a person's drinking patterns are safe, risky, or harmful. Answering these questions will take only a minute, and will give results based on age, gender, and drinking patterns.

PHOTO CREDITS

PAGE

17: Frank Nash/Alamy
18: Rita Maas/Getty Images
24: Getty Images
25: Alinari Archives/Corbis
31: Time & Life Pictures/
    Getty Images
32: Bettmann/Corbis
34: Bettmann/Corbis
35: AP Images
37: AP Images
41: Getty Images
44: David Young-Wolff/
    Getty Images
53: Getty Images
67: Newscom
73: AP Images
74: AP Images
77: AP Images
78: Mark E. Gibson/Corbis
80: Medical-on-line/Alamy

INDEX

ABOUT THE AUTHORS

Minneapolis-area journalist **TERRI PETERSON SMITH** writes about science, health, and the outdoors for national magazines, university publications, and Web sites. Smith has also coauthored several middle-grade science textbooks. She was the winner of the 2008 Michael E. DeBakey Journalism Award from the Foundation for Biomedical Research.

Series introduction author **RONALD J. BROGAN** is the Bureau Chief for the New York City office of D.A.R.E. (Drug Abuse Resistance Education) America, where he trains and coordinates more than 100 New York City police officers in program-related activities. He also serves as a D.A.R.E. regional director for Oregon, Connecticut, Massachusetts, Maine, New Hampshire, New York, Rhode Island, and Vermont. In 1997, Brogan retired from the U.S. Drug Enforcement Administration (DEA), where he served as a special agent for 26 years. He holds bachelor's and master's degrees in criminal justice from the City University of New York.